ADVANCED SHOTOKAN
KARATE KATAS

ADVANCED SHOTOKAN
KARATE KATAS

By
John van Weenen 5th Dan
Chief Instructor:
Traditional Association of Shotokan Karate (G.B.)

Published by
Paul Hooley and Associates

ABOUT THE SERIES

Volume one of Advanced Shotokan Karate Katas is the first of three volumes covering in detail twenty two of the more advanced Katas as practised in the Shotokan style.

We will examine Katas such as *Chinte*, with its Chinese Kempo origins and multitude of circular techniques, and *Tekki Sandan*, a Kata sometimes neglected by senior grades, with its short, sharp, intricate moves, which stretch the practitioners ability to "Kime", to the limit.

Intermediate Katas such as *Enpi, Jion, Jitte, Kanku-Dai, Tekki Shodan, Tekki Nidan* and *Sochin* will all receive detailed attention, as too will *Bassai-Sho, Kanku-Sho* and *Gankaku,* the Kata which brings to mind a crane

standing on one foot on a rock — ready to attack.

Meikyo, previously known as *Rohai* until renamed by Funakoshi Sensei, embodies many advanced techniques, none more so than "Sankaku – Tobi" (Triangular jump) which theoretically takes place on a cliff edge, whereby the performer launches himself into space in order to avoid an attack and returns to terra firma, dealing with the opponent in an appropriate manner.

The series concludes with *Nijushiho, Seienchin, Unsu, Wankan* and *Gojushiho.*

Eliminating directional problems has been overcome by "The Compass System" which will be used extensively, and the overall series should prove beneficial to student and instructor alike.

The Beginners Guide to Shotokan Karate

Written in plain English and extensively illustrated, **The Beginners Guide to Shotokan Karate** is the most comprehensive, easy to follow textbook yet produced for Western students.

This high class production, thread sewn for longer life, contains 280 action-packed pages of over 1200 photographs, showing a complete breakdown of 38 basic punches, kicks, strikes and blocks.

The Kata section illustrates and explains in detail Taikyoku Sho Dan and the five Heian Katas, showing every intermediate, front and side view, together with six segments on application techniques.

Go Hon, Sambon and Ippon Kumite are fully covered in this expert work which will give the seasoned student as well as the beginner a greater and fuller understanding of Karate-Dō, particularly the system known as Shotokan.

Advanced Shotokan Karate Katas will comprise of the following:

Volume 1	Volume 2	Volume 3
Bassai-Dai	**Wankan**	**Kanku-Sho**
Chinte	**Ji'in**	**Enpi**
Jion	**Sochin**	**Unsu**
Jitte	**Kanku Dai**	**Seienchin**
Tekki Shodan	**Gankaku**	**Hangetsu**
Tekki Nidan	**Meikyo**	**Nijushiho**
Tekki Sandan	**Bassai Sho**	**Gojushiho Dai**
		Gojushiho Sho

Available from W H Smith, Foyles and most good book shops or direct from: Giko Ltd, 537 Stratford Road, Sparkhill, Birmingham B11 4LP, England. Tel. 021-773 9247. Send cheque or postal order for £7.95 plus 95p postage and packing.

Acknowledgements to Sensei van Weenen's Assistants in Kata Applications:

Gursharan Sahota	**3rd Dan**
Andrew Balfour	**2nd Dan**
Terance McNelly	**2nd Dan**
Mattison Dass	**2nd Dan**
Stephen Watson	**2nd Dan**
Bernard Coppen	**2nd Dan**
John Caves	**2nd Dan**

Publishers Note:

Since November 1982, The Beginners Guide to Shotokan Karate has sold over 25,000 copies in the UK alone and is currently the best selling book on the Shotokan style.

FOREWORD

It is very difficult for a westerner to learn karate. To be sure, he or she can learn the moves well enough but that is a long way from learning the art. For karate *is* an art. In its purest form, karate is an expression of Japanese culture; that same culture which has produced the beauty of the tea ceremony and the ritual suicide of seppuku.

Karate, like the Japanese character, is enigmatic. On the surface, it is a system of powerful kicks, punches and strikes that can shatter bricks. It is also an exciting yet safe form of combat sport. But it is a fact that you may train to perform the most amazing feats of breaking, or win the world karate championships, yet know nothing of the way of karate.

True karate trains the mind. It is a vehicle for improving the character through physical effort and perseverance. Therefore the techniques of karate are in themselves unimportant; they are only a means to an end.

This is not to say that one should regard karate technique with contempt. It is through practice and application of technique that the inner meaning of karate is appreciated. Yet success in mastering technique is not the ultimate achievement to be sought.

Technique provides the means by which a knowledge of karate is gained and kata is the most important form of technique training. To the Okinawan masters who introduced their art to the Japanese mainland, it was the only form.

Nowadays, other aspects of training such as competition and sparring have assumed an exaggerated importance. As a result, we have become fixated upon technique and the deeper meaning of karate lost.

This is why I appreciate the work done by John van Weenen, in seeking to re-establish the true meaning of karate through the medium of kata. Because the book is well researched and presented, it is a must for all karateka, regardless of their style and level of practice.

John has drawn our attention back to this primary issue of karate without which we would remain students, copying but never understanding.

David Mitchell,
Directing Committee European Karate Union
Directing Committee World Union of Karate Organisations

First published: March 1987

Reprinted February 1988

By the same author: The Beginners Guide to Shotokan Karate

ISBN 0 905095 26 X

© *Copyright 1987* John van Weenen

Published by: Paul Hooley & Associates

Printed by: Newnorth-Burt Ltd, Newnorth House, College Street, Kempston, Bedford MK42 8NA

Photography: Trevor Yorke

CONTENTS

"Therefore I say: know the enemy and know yourself; in a hundred battles you will never be in peril.

However —

To win one hundred victories in one hundred battles is not the highest skill. To subdue the enemy without fighting is the highest skill."

Gichin Funakoshi.

GICHIN FUNAKOSHI

The father of modern day Karate, who was a scholar of the Chinese Classics as well as a Karate Master. He was born in Shuri, Okinawa Prefecture, in 1868 and died in Tokyo in 1957.

Dedicated
to My Teacher
Hirokazu Kanazawa

To be elated at success
and disappointed at failure,
is to be the child of circumstances.

How can such a one be called
the master of himself.

Tut-Tut.
Chinese Philosopher.

BASSAI DAI

抜塞大

INTRODUCTION

Literally translated "Bassai" means "to storm a Castle," thus implying strong spirit, forcefulness and an underlying will to succeed. The repeated changing of the blocking arms represent the feeling of shifting from a disadvantageous position to an advantageous one. Continuous attacks with techniques like "Yama Zuki" suggest a will to penetrate the opponents defences.

There are two "Bassai" — "Dai" and "Sho". Being the more elementary of the two, Bassai Dai is generally taught before Bassai Sho.

The system for explaining the Kata is as follows:

On page Four you will find a schematic diagram of Bassai Dai, and a picture of the camera used to photograph all the main movements which appear at the top of the following pages. The camera position remains constant and the practitioner begins and ends his Kata facing the camera. If in retreat, when his movements are obscured by his back view, we have photographed him from the side or front and this has been clearly marked.

For many years now, Shotokan Karate students have been taught to more forward, back, to left or right, or to "45°". This applies to basics, Kata and all six forms of basic Kumite.

In this book, to assist in the explanation of Kata, as far as DIRECTION is concerned, I have likened these moves to the points of the compass.

At the top left hand side of page Four will be found an illustration of a compass showing the four cardinal points — North, South, East and West — together with the four lesser ones of South East, South West, etc. Eight positions in all — the same eight that cover almost every Shotokan move taught today.

On the top right hand side of the page is a simplified version showing the eight directions. With the practitioner standing in the centre, facing the camera, forward is "One," back is "Two", his left is "Three", and his right "Four".

The first thirty nine movements of "Bassai Dai" are in one of four directions.

The final three moves of the Kata are at angles of 45°, i.e. five, eight and seven.

Once this simple eight point system has been grasped, the most advanced Kata can be easily understood — directionally speaking.

To summarize then — the photograph at the top of the page is the completed move.

The photographs in the centre of the page show the completed moves — possibly at different angles, to aid understanding — plus the midway points. Finally, the practical application is shown at the bottom of the page and a complete summary of "Bassai Dai" appears on page 28.

There is no substitute for a good teacher and this book is merely intended to complement that teaching — not replace it.

The following ten elements of Kata, as taught by Kanazawa Sensei, should be borne in mind at all times. Without them, the Kata will be meaningless.

YOI NO KISIN — the spirit of getting ready. The concentration of will and mind against the opponent as a preliminary to the movements of the Kata.

INYO — the active and passive. Always keeping in mind both attack and defence.

CHIKARA NO KYOJAKU — the manner of using strength. The degree of power used for each movement and position in Kata.

WAZA NO KANKYU — the speed of movement. The speed used for each movement and position in Kata.

TAI NO SHINSHUKU — the degree of expansion or contraction. The degree of expansion or contraction of the body in each movement and position in Kata.

KOKYU — breathing. Breath control related to the posture and movement in Kata*.

TYAKUGAN — the aiming points. In Kata you must keep the purpose of the movement in mind.

KIAI — shouting. Shouting at set points in Kata to demonstrate the martial spirit.

KEITAI NO HOJI — correct positioning. Correct positioning in movement and stance.

ZANSHIN — remaining on guard. Remaining on guard at the completion of the Kata (i.e. back to 'Yoi') until told to relax 'Enoy'.

*N.B. KOKYU — Breathing in Kata plays a very important part towards its correct execution. Inhalation takes place via the nose and exhalation through the mouth. In the following Kata, where a "sequence" of techniques occurs, inhalation is immediately followed by exhalation spread over the number of techniques involved, which often are performed in rapid succession.

SCHEMATIC DIAGRAM OF BASSAI DAI
AND DIRECTIONAL ANALYSIS

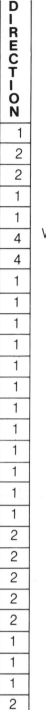

MOVE	DIRECTION
1	1
2	2
3	2
4	1
5	1
6	4
7	4
8	1
9	1
10	1
11	1
12	1
13	1
14	1
15	1
16	1
17	1
18	1
19	1
20	2
21	2
22	2
23	2
24	2
25	1
26	1
27	1
28	2
29	4
30	4
31	4
32	2
33	2
34	2
35	2
36	2
37	2
38	1
39	1
40	5
41	8
42	7

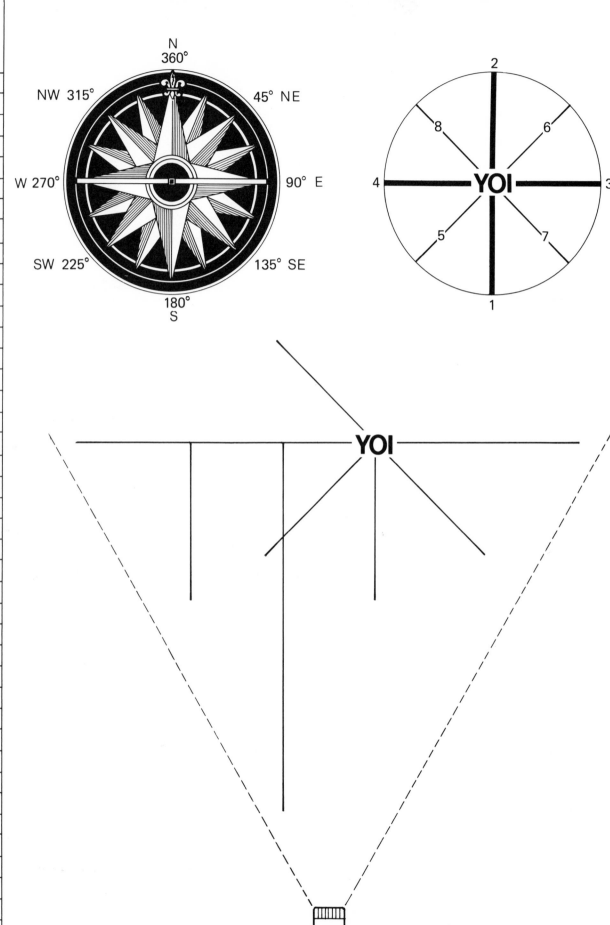

SHIZENTAI

YOI

SHIZENTAI

MIDWAY

YOI

The Bow (Rei) has not been shown here but it is assumed that all Karateka reaching the level of Bassai Dai, will be aware of its significance both before and at the conclusion of the Kata.

After the "Rei", move the right foot into the Shizentai position, simultaneously crossing the arms in front of the body.

To move into the "Yoi" position, move the right foot across to the left and move "both hands" to the centre of your body. The left hand clasping or wrapping around the right fist.

MOVEMENT 1	MOVEMENT 2

MIGI UCHI UDE UKE

HIDARI CHŪDAN UCHI UKE

YOI

MIDWAY

MIGI UCHI UDE UKE

MIDWAY

MOVEMENT 1
Right inside forearm block

STANCE: Kōsa Dachi — cross legged stance.

SHIFT 1: Swing the arms to the left side of the body at the same time step forward with the right foot into a long forward stance, sharply bringing the rear foot up behind the front foot in Kosa Dachi. The right arm blocks and the left palm augments it.

SPEED: Fast with focus.

BREATHING: Fast in through nose, fast out through mouth.

DIRECTION:

MOVEMENT 2
Left inside forearm block

STANCE: Zenkutsu Dachi — Forward stance.

SHIFT 2: Move the left leg behind the right and turn 180° into a left forward stance.

DIRECTION:

SPEED: Fast with focus.

BREATHING: Fast, in through nose, out through mouth.

BLOCKING A LUNGE PUNCH

BLOCKING A LUNGE PUNCH

CHŪDAN UCHI UKE-GYAKU HANMI

CHŪDAN SOTO UKE-GYAKU HANMI

**HIDARI CHŪDAN
UCHI UKE**
FRONT VIEW

MIDWAY

**CHŪDAN UCHI UKE-
GYAKU HANMI**
FRONT VIEW

MIDWAY

MOVEMENT 3
**Right middle inside forearm
block in the reverse position**

STANCE: Zenkutsu Dachi —
Forward stance.

SHIFT 3: Block on the spot,
twisting the hips and body 90° —
Gyaku Hanmi (Reverse body
position). At the same time pull the
front foot back one foot's length to
enable the rear hip to be applied
properly.

BREATHING: Fast, in through
nose out through mouth.

SPEED: Fast with focus.

DIRECTION:

MOVEMENT 4
**Middle outside forearm block in
reverse body position**

STANCE: Right Zenkutsu Dachi
— Forward stance.

SHIFT 4: Move the right leg
behind and across and turn 180°
performing an outside block in
Gyaku Hanmi (reverse body
position).

SPEED: Fast with focus.

BREATHING: Fast, in through
nose out through mouth.

DIRECTION:

BLOCKING A REVERSE PUNCH

BLOCKING A LUNGE PUNCH

MOVEMENT 5

MIGI CHŪDAN UCHI UKE

MOVEMENT 6

MIGI CHŪDAN SOTO UKE

4

MIDWAY

CHŪDAN SOTO UKE
GYAKU HANMI

MOVEMENT 5
Right middle inside forearm block

STANCE: Right Zenkutsu Dachi (forward stance).

SHIFT 5: From the Gyaku Hanmi position. Twist the hips and upper body 90° and execute a right inside forearm block.

SPEED: Fast with focus.

BREATHING: Fast, in through nose out through mouth.

1

5

MIGI CHŪDAN UCHI
UKE

DIRECTION:

1

MOVEMENT 6
Right middle outside forearm block

STANCE: Right Zenkutsu Dachi (forward stance).

SHIFT 6: Pull the right foot back and perform a right scooping block, pulling up into Heisoku Dachi. From there, step forward with the right leg performing a right outside forearm block.

SPEED: Fast with focus.

BREATHING: Fast, in through nose out through mouth.

DIRECTION:

4

MIDWAY

MIDWAY

2

LIFTING AND THROWING

CHŪDAN UCHI UKE-GYAKU HANMI

KOSHI GAMAE-SHIZENTAI

MIGI CHŪDAN SOTO UKE

MIDWAY

CHŪDAN UCHI UKE GYAKU HANMI

MIDWAY

MOVEMENT 7
Left middle inside forearm block in reverse body position

STANCE: Right forward stance.

SHIFT 7: Block on the spot pulling the front foot back one foot's length to enable the opposite hip to come forward. The body should twist 90° together with the hips.

SPEED: Fast with focus.

BREATHING: Fast, in through nose out through mouth.

DIRECTION:

MOVEMENT 8
Preparatory position

STANCE: Shizentai, Natural stance (prepared).

SHIFT 8: Assume the Koshi Gamae position by moving the left leg.

SPEED: Slowly, about 2 seconds.

BREATHING: Slowly in through nose.

DIRECTION:

BLOCKING A LUNGE PUNCH

COUNTERING WITH A JABBING PUNCH (KIZAMI ZUKI)

HIDARI CHŪDAN TATE SHUTŌ UKE

MIGI CHŪDAN ZUKI-SHIZENTAI

KOSHI GAMAE-SHIZENTAI

MIDWAY

HIDARI CHŪDAN TATE SHUTŌ UKE

MIDWAY

MOVEMENT 9
Middle vertical knife hand block

STANCE: Hachiji Dachi (natural stance).

SHIFT 9: Swing left arm in an arc blocking a Chudan punch.

SPEED: Slowly about two seconds.

BREATHING: Out slowly.

DIRECTION:

MOVEMENT 10
Middle right straight punch

STANCE: Hachiji Dachi (natural stance).

SHIFT 10: Perform a middle area straight punch.

SPEED: Fast with focus.

BREATHING: In fully through nose and half out through mouth.

DIRECTION:

BLOCKING

PUNCHING

MIGI CHŪDAN UCHI UKE

HIDARI CHŪDAN ZUKI

MIGI CHŪDAN ZUKI SHIZENTAI

10

MIDWAY

11

MIGI CHŪDAN UCHI UKE

MIDWAY

MOVEMENT 11
Middle right inside forearm block

STANCE: Short forward stance.

SHIFT 11: Bring the right fist across to touch the left upper arm keeping the body square on — twist the body and hips at the same time as blocking.

SPEED: Fast with focus.

BREATHING: Other half of breath out through mouth.

DIRECTION:

1

MOVEMENT 12
Middle left straight punch

STANCE: Shizentai.

SHIFT 12: Whilst punching with the left hand twist the body straight — square on to the front — Direction 1.

SPEED: Fast with focus.

BREATHING: Breath in through nose and half out whilst punching.

DIRECTION:

1

3

BLOCKING

4

PUNCHING

HIDARI CHŪDAN UCHI UKE

MIGI CHŪDAN SHUTŌ UKE

HIDARI CHŪDAN ZUKI SHIZENTAI

MIDWAY

HIDARI CHŪDAN UCHI UKE

MIDWAY

MOVEMENT 13
Middle left inside forearm block

STANCE: Short forward stance.

SHIFT 13: Move the left fist across to the right upper arm and whilst blocking, twist the body and hips. The left hip should be forward into the block with the right leg bent at the knee.

SPEED: Fast with focus.

BREATHING: Other half of breath out through mouth.

DIRECTION:

MOVEMENT 14
Right middle knife hand block

STANCE: Back stance (Kōkutsu-Dachi).

SHIFT 14: Move the right hand behind the left ear and the right foot to the left one, then step forward with the right foot and perform Migi Chudan Shuto Uke.

SPEED: Fast with focus.

BREATHING: In through nose out through mouth.

DIRECTION:

HIDARI CHŪDAN SHUTŌ UKE

MIGI CHŪDAN SHUTŌ UKE

**MIGI CHŪDAN
SHUTŌ UKE**

MIDWAY

**HIDARI CHŪDAN
SHUTŌ UKE**

MIDWAY

MOVEMENT 15
Left middle knife hand block

STANCE: Back stance (Kōkutsu-Dachi)

SHIFT 15: Step forward from a right back stance into a left back stance simultaneously executing a left knife hand block. Care must be taken to keep the weight back when proceeding forward.

SPEED: Fast with focus.

BREATHING: In through nose, out through mouth.

DIRECTION:

MOVEMENT 16
Right middle knife hand block

STANCE: Back stance (Kōkutsu-Dachi).

SHIFT 16: Shift forward from a left knife hand block into a right knife hand block.

SPEED: Fast with focus (kime).

BREATHING: In via the nose and out by the mouth.

DIRECTION:

BLOCKING   BLOCKING

HIDARI CHŪDAN SHUTŌ UKE

MIGI TSUKAMI UKE HIDARI SOETE

16

MIGI CHŪDAN SHUTŌ UKE

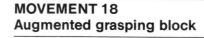

MIDWAY

17

HIDARI CHŪDAN SHUTŌ UKE

MIDWAY

MOVEMENT 17
Left middle knife hand block

STANCE: Back stance (Kōkutsu Dachi).

SHIFT 17: Step back into a left middle knife hand block.

SPEED: Fast with focus. This movement follows movement 16 immediately with no pause in between.

BREATHING: In through nose, out through mouth.

DIRECTION: 1. This technique is performed facing forward although stepping back.

MOVEMENT 18
Augmented grasping block

STANCE: Forward stance (Zenkutsu Dachi)

SHIFT 18: Move the right foot over to the right about two feet and change from a back to a forward stance. At the same time, keeping the left hand in the Shutō position, take the right hand up and under the left, the pull down as indicated above.

SPEED: Slowly, about four seconds.

BREATHING: In through nose, out through mouth.

DIRECTION:

1

SHIFTING THE ATTACKING ARM

GEDAN KESAGE

HIDARI CHŪDAN SHUTŌ UKE

**MIGI TSUKAMI UKE
HIDARI SOETE**   MIDWAY   **GEDAN KESAGE**   MIDWAY

MOVEMENT 19
Lower thrust kick to knee joint

STANCE: On one leg.

SHIFT 19: Draw the right knee up between the arms and simultaneously pull both fists to the chest as you kick to the knee joint with Gedan Kekomi.

SPEED: Fast with Kiai.

BREATHING: In through nose, out through mouth.

DIRECTION:

MOVEMENT 20
Left middle knife hand block

STANCE: Back stance (Kōkutsu Dachi).

SHIFT 20: Bring the kicking foot back to the left knee at the same time extend the right hand palm down in the direction of 2. and cup the right ear with the left hand. Fall back into a left knife hand block.

SPEED: Fast with focus.

BREATHING: In through nose, out through mouth.

DIRECTION:

GRASPING   HOLDING   PULLING THE ARM — DISLOCATING THE KNEE   **15**

MIGI CHŪDAN SHUTŌ UKE

MOROTE AGE UKE

HIDARI CHŪDAN SHUTŌ UKE FRONT VIEW

MIDWAY FRONT VIEW

MIGI CHŪDAN SHUTŌ UKE FRONT VIEW

MIDWAY FRONT VIEW

MIDWAY FRONT VIEW

MOVEMENT 21
Middle right knife hand block.

STANCE: Back stance (Kōkutsu Dachi)

SHIFT 21: Step forward from a left back stance into a right back stance and in so doing, perform a right knife hand block to the mid-section.

SPEED: Fast with focus

BREATHING: In through nose, out through mouth.

DIRECTION:

MOVEMENT 22

STANCE: Informal attention stance (Heisoku Dachi)

SHIFT 22: Pull the right foot back to the left into Heisoku Dachi. Keep the left hand open and bring the open right hand to it (side by side, palms up). Start to raise the arms, making a fist with both hands and as the fists pass the face, let the elbows turn out as you complete Morote Age Uke.

SPEED: Slowly — 4/5 seconds, increasing tension.

BREATHING: Breathing in through nose slowly all the way.

ATTACKER GRABS LAPELS

BREAKING GRIP

CHŪDAN TETTSUI HASAMI UCHI

MIGI CHŪDAN OI ZUKI

MOROTE AGE UKE
FRONT VIEW

MIDWAY FRONT VIEW

**CHŪDAN TETTSUI
HASAMI UCHI**
FRONT VIEW

**MIGI CHŪDAN
OI ZUKI**
FRONT VIEW

**MOVEMENT 23
Middle double hammer
fist strike**

STANCE: Forward stance
(Zenkutsu Dachi)

SHIFT 23: Pull the arms strongly

apart, whilst lifting the right knee high and move forward into a right forward stance. At the same time describe a semi circle with both fists and as the double bottom fist strike is completed, the fists should be level with the sides of the body.

SPEED: Fast with focus

BREATHING: Half
out through mouth.

DIRECTION:

**MOVEMENT 24
Right middle lunge punch**

STANCE: Forward stance
(Zenkutsu Dachi)

SHIFT 24: Slide both feet forward and perform a right middle lunge punch.

SPEED: Fast with focus (Kime)

BREATHING:
Other half of breath
out through mouth.

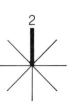

DIRECTION:

STRIKING TO BODY

PUNCHING

**HIDARI NAGASHI UKE
MIGI GEDAN SHUTŌ UCHI**

MANJI GAMAE

**MIGI CHŪDAN
OI ZUKI**

MIDWAY

**HIDARI NAGASHI UKE
MIGI GEDAN
SHUTŌ UCHI**

MIDWAY

MOVEMENT 25
Left sweeping block and right lower knife hand strike.

STANCE: Forward stance (Zenkutsu Dachi)

SHIFT 25: Move the left leg behind the right and turn 180° firstly blocking a Mae Geri with left lower Shutō Uke, then with the same hand, block an Oi Zuki to the face and immediately strike the testicles by performing a right knife hand strike.

SPEED: Fast with Focus

BREATHING: In through nose, out through mouth fast.

DIRECTION:

MOVEMENT 26
Manji Gamae

STANCE: Informal attention stance (Heisoku Dachi)

SHIFT 26: Slowly pull the left leg back to the right into Heisoku Dachi performing a Gedan Barai with the left arm and an upper block to the head.

SPEED: Slowly, about 3 to 4 seconds.

BREATHING: Slowly in through nose.

DIRECTION:

BLOCKING

BLOCKING AND ATTACKING

BEING GRABBED

MIGI GEDAN BARAI

HIDARI CHŪDAN HAISHU UKE

MANJI GAMAE
26

MIDWAY

MIGI GEDAN BARAI
27

MIDWAY
SIDE VIEW

MOVEMENT 27
Right lower block

STANCE: Straddle stance (Kiba Dachi).

SHIFT 27: Pivot on the left foot, swing the right foot high and round and perform a stamping kick as Gedan Barai is completed in straddle stance.

SPEED: Fast with focus.

BREATHING: Out quickly through mouth.

DIRECTION:

1

MOVEMENT 28
Left middle back hand block

STANCE: Straddle stance (Kiba Dachi).

SHIFT 28: Turn the head 180°, bring the left fist above the right hip and the right arm stretching in the direction of the block. Remain in straddle stance and perform Chūdan Back hand block as illustrated.

SPEED: Slowly — about 5 seconds.

BREATHING: Quickly in through nose — slowly out through mouth.

DIRECTION:

2

4

BREAKING GRIP

1

BLOCKING A PUNCH

MIGI CHŪDAN ENPI UCHI

MIGI GEDAN BARAI HIDARI SOETE

**HIDARI CHŪDAN
HAISHU UKE**
SIDE VIEW

MIDWAY
SIDE VIEW

MIGI ENPI UCHI
SIDE VIEW

MIDWAY
SIDE VIEW

**MOVEMENT 29
Right middle elbow strike**

STANCE: Straddle stance (Kiba Dachi).

SHIFT 29: Without moving the arms, swing the right leg round performing Mikazuki Geri — continue round and execute Chūdan Enpi Uchi in straddle stance.

SPEED: Fast with focus.

BREATHING: In through nose, out through mouth.

DIRECTION:

**MOVEMENT 30
Right lower augmented downwards block**

STANCE: Straddle stance (Kiba Dachi).

SHIFT 30: Perform a right downward block. The left fist presses vertically on the upper right arm.

SPEED: Fast with focus.

BREATHING: Fast in through nose — half out through mouth.

DIRECTION:

BLOCKING A KICK   PUNCHING TO THE GROIN

MIGI GEDAN BARAI HIDARI SOETE

KOSHI GAMAE

MIGI GEDAN BARAI HIDARI SOETE
SIDE VIEW

HIDARI GEDAN BARAI MIGI SOETE
SIDE VIEW

MIGI GEDAN BARAI HIDARI SOETE
SIDE VIEW

KOSHI GAMAE

MOVEMENT 31
Right lower augmented downward block

STANCE: Straddle stance (Kiba Dachi).

SHIFT 31: The same as movement 30, but in between 30 and 31, the left arm blocks Gedan Barai with the right fist vertically pressing on the left upper arm.

SPEED: Fast with focus.

BREATHING: Over the two movements let the remaining half breath out through the mouth.

DIRECTION: 4

MOVEMENT 32
Koshi Gamae

STANCE: Forward stance (Zenkutsu Dachi).

SHIFT 32: Move the right leg back two feet and twist 90° into a right forward stance, simultaneously bringing the left fist to the left hip with the right fist on top of it in the vertical position. Hips must be at 45°.

SPEED: Fast but relaxed.

BREATHING: In quickly through nose.

DIRECTION: 2

N.B.

MOVEMENTS 30-31

The finishing position of these two movements is identical, however, the midway point between them is a left downward block performed with the right vertical fist resting on the upper left arm. This has been shown in the central photographs but is not a main movement in the Kata.

YAMA ZUKI

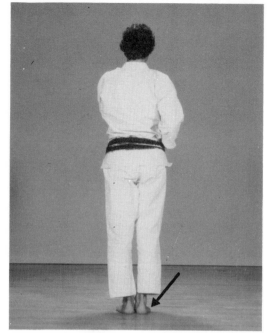

KOSHI GAMAE

KOSHI GAMAE
SIDE VIEW

MIDWAY
SIDE VIEW

YAMA ZUKI
SIDE VIEW

MIDWAY
SIDE VIEW

MOVEMENT 33
U punch (Yama Zuki)

STANCE: Forward stance (Zenkutsu Dachi).

SHIFT 33: Perform a U punch by leaning the body forward and thrusting both fists out. Keep the arms bent so that both fists remain in a vertical line. The right fist is turned palm up.

SPEED: Fast with focus.

BREATHING: Out quickly through mouth.

DIRECTION:

MOVEMENT 34
Koshi Gamae

STANCE: Heisoku Dachi.

SHIFT 34: Slowly bring the right foot to the left and the fists to the right side of the body with the left one vertically over the right.

SPEED: Slowly, about 2 seconds.

BREATHING: Slowly in through nose.

DIRECTION:

BLOCKING A KICK

YAMA ZUKI

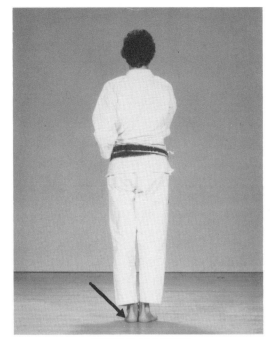

KOSHI GAMAE

KOSHI GAMAE
SIDE VIEW

HARAI FUMIKOMI
SIDE VIEW

YAMA ZUKI
SIDE VIEW

MIDWAY
SIDE VIEW

MOVEMENT 35
U Punch (Yama Zuki)

STANCE: Forward stance.

SHIFT 35: Swing the left leg in an arc and perform Fumikomi simultaneously punching with a U punch as you land in a forward stance.

SPEED: Fast with focus.

BREATHING: Out quickly through mouth.

DIRECTION:

MOVEMENT 36
Koshi Gamae

STANCE: Heisoku Dachi.

SHIFT 36: Pull the left leg back slowly to the right and bring the fists to the left hand side of the body with the right one vertically on top.

SPEED: Slowly — about 2 seconds.

BREATHING: Slowly — in through nose.

DIRECTION:

COUNTER ATTACKING WITH A "U" PUNCH

YAMA ZUKI

MIGI GEDAN SUKUI UKE

KOSHI GAMAE
SIDE VIEW

HARAI FUMIKOMI
SIDE VIEW

YAMA ZUKI
SIDE VIEW

MIDWAY

MOVEMENT 37
U Punch (Yama Zuki)

STANCE: Forward stance (Zenkutsu Dachi).

SHIFT 37: Same as movement 33.

SPEED: Fast with focus.

BREATHING: Fast out through mouth.

DIRECTION:

MOVEMENT 38
Right lower scooping block

STANCE: Forward stance (Zenkutsu Dachi).

SHIFT 38: Position the arms as illustrated, swinging the right arm down and perform a scooping action similar to Uchi Uke. The stance changes through 180° at the end of the technique as the hips twist to strengthen the block.

SPEED: Fast with focus.

BREATHING: In through nose, out through mouth.

DIRECTION:

MIDWAY

CATCHING THE LEG

TWISTING AND

HIDARI GEDAN SUKUI UKE

MIGI CHŪDAN SHUTO UKE

MIGI GEDAN SUKUI UKE

MIDWAY

HIDARI GEDAN SUKUI UKE

MIDWAY

MIDWAY

BREATHING: In through nose, out through mouth.

DIRECTION:

1

MOVEMENT 40
Right middle knife hand block

STANCE: Back stance (Kōkutsu Dachi).

SHIFT 40: Bring the left foot up half a step behind the right one and step forward at a 45° angle with the right leg and perform a right knife hand block.

SPEED: Fast with focus.

BREATHING: In through nose, out through mouth.

DIRECTION:

MOVEMENT 39
Left lower scooping block

STANCE: Forward stance (Zenkutsu Dachi).

SHIFT 39: Raise the left arm up as illustrated and repeat the preceeding movement but in a reverse direction.

SPEED: Fast with focus.

3
SCOOPING

5

MIGI CHŪDAN SHUTŌ UKE

KIAI

HIDARI CHŪDAN SHUTŌ UKE

40

**MIGI CHŪDAN
SHUTŌ UKE**

MIDWAY

41

**MIGI CHŪDAN
SHUTŌ UKE**

MIDWAY

MOVEMENT 41
Right middle knife hand block

STANCE: Back stance (Kōkutsu Dachi).

SHIFT 41: Maintain the right knife hand block from the previous movement and pivot 90° on the left foot, pushing the previous attack to one side. This technique is not an actual block but a preparatory position before the final technique and kiai.

SPEED: Slowly about 1-2 seconds.

BREATHING: In and out slowly.

DIRECTION: 8. Head facing direction 7.

MOVEMENT 42
Left middle knife hand block

STANCE: Back stance (Kōkutsu Dachi).

SHIFT 42: Bring the right foot to the left one, left hand by the right ear and right hand extended forward palm down and step into a left back stance performing a left knife hand block with kiai.

1

BLOCKING A PUNCH

2

PUSHING THE ATTACKING
ARM ASIDE

3

BLOCKING A PUNCH

YAME

SHIZENTAI

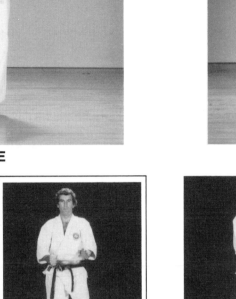

**HIDARI CHŪDAN
SHUTŌ UKE**

MIDWAY

YAME

SHIZENTAI

SPEED: Fast.

BREATHING: In fast through nose, out fast through mouth.

DIRECTION:

7

KNIFE HAND STRIKE
TO THE NECK

After Kiai, pause for a second then pull the left foot back to the right at the same time clasping the right fist with the left hand. At this point the feet are parallel in Heisoku Dachi, the eyes are looking straight ahead, the body is relaxed but still on guard, for the Kata is not yet finished.

From this position, move the right leg into Shizentai simultaneously crossing the arms in front of the body in a protective manner — finally, move the right leg up to the left one, bring the hands to the sides, and bow. (Rei).

Kata begins and ends with courtesy — as too, does Karate-Dō.

BASSAI DAI

REI

SHIZENTAI

YOI

1

6

7

8

9

14

15

16

17

22

23

24

25

30

31

32

33

38

39

40

41

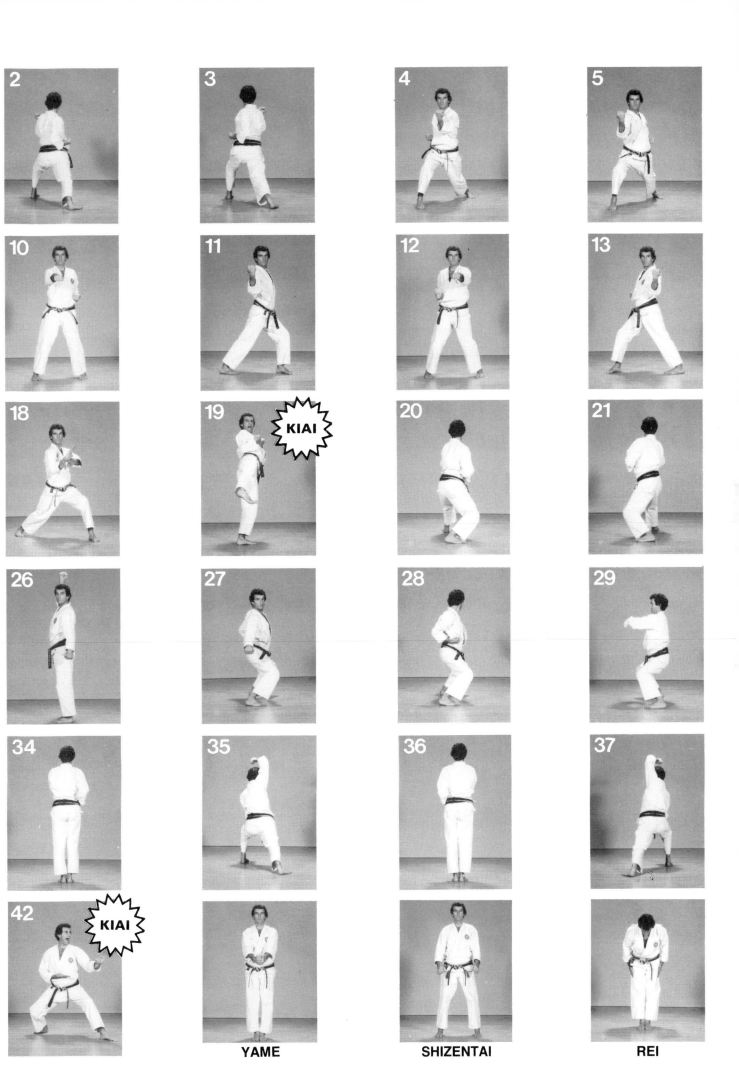

YAME

SHIZENTAI

REI

"Whatever you do in the world
will always come back to you.

This is the law of Karma.

If you do good — you will end up
Having good done unto you.

If you do bad — always it
will return.

It does not appear immediately;
But ultimately it rules your life."

CHINTE

珍手

INTRODUCTION

Documented evidence is scant but the one thing we can be reasonably certain of, is that Chinte has come down to us from Chinese Kempo. Renamed "Shoin" by Funakoshi, but not generally adhered to today, Chinte was retained by some Masters of Okinawa-Te for its wide circular movements. These movements are excellent for exercising the shoulders and when practised by women, give increased power, due to the centrifugal effect generated by the arms pivoting at the shoulders.

Chinte's hand techniques are artistic and the almost total absence of kicking is significant.

The system for explaining the Kata is as follows:

On page 34 you will find a schematic diagram of Chinte and a picture of the camera used to photograph all the main movements which appear at the top of the following pages. The camera position remains constant and the practitioner begins and ends his Kata facing the camera. If in retreat, when his movements are obscured by his back view, we have photographed him from the side or front and this has been clearly marked.

For many years now, throughout Shotokan Karate, students have been taught to move forward, back, to left or right, or to "45°". This applies to basics, Kata and all six forms of basic Kumite.

In this book, to assist in the explanation of Kata, as far as DIRECTION is concerned, I have likened these moves to the points of the compass.

At the top left hand side of page 34 will be found a photograph of a compass showing the four cardinal points of North, South, East and West, together with the four lesser ones of South East, South West, etc. Eight in all — the same eight that cover almost every Shotokan move taught today.

On the top right hand side of the page is a simplified version showing the eight directions. With the practitioner standing in the centre, facing the camera, forward is "One", back is "Two", his left is "Three", and his right "Four".

Once this simple eight point system has been grasped, the most advanced Kata can be easily understood — directionally speaking.

To summarize then — the photograph at the top of the page is the completed move.

The photographs in the centre of the page show the completed moves, possibly at different angles, to aid understanding, plus the midway points. Finally, the practical application is shown at the bottom of the page and a complete summary of Chinte appears on Page 56.

There is no substitute for a good teacher and this book is merely intended to complement that teaching — not replace it.

The following ten elements of Kata, as taught by Kanazawa Sensei, should be borne in mind at all times. Without them, the Kata will be meaningless.

YOI NO KISIN — the spirit of getting ready. The concentration of will and mind against the opponent as a preliminary to the movements of the Kata.

INYO — the active and passive. Always keeping in mind both attack and defence.

CHIKARA NO KYOJAKU — the manner of using strength. The degree of power used for each movement and position in Kata.

WAZA NO KANKYU — the speed of movement. The speed used for each movement and position in Kata.

TAI NO SHINSHUKU — the degree of expansion or contraction. The degree of expansion or contraction of the body in each movement and position in Kata.

KOKYU — breathing. Breath control related to the posture and movement in Kata*.

TYAKUGAN — the aiming points. In Kata you must keep the purpose of the movement in mind.

KIAI — shouting. Shouting at set points in Kata to demonstrate the martial spirit.

KEITAI NO HOJI — correct positioning. Correct positioning in movement and stance.

ZANSHIN — remaining on guard. Remaining on guard at the completion of the Kata (i.e. back to 'Yoi') until told to relax 'Enoy'.

*N.B. KOKYU — Breathing in Kata plays a very important part towards its correct execution. Inhalation takes place via the nose and exhalation through the mouth. In the following Kata, where a "sequence" of techniques occurs, inhalation is immediately followed by exhalation spread over the number of techniques involved, which often are performed in rapid succession.

珍手

SCHEMATIC DIAGRAM OF CHINTE AND DIRECTIONAL ANALYSIS

MOVE	DIRECTION
1	4
2	1
3	3
4	4
5	2
6	2
7	2
8	2
9	2
10	2
11	1
12	1
13	1
14	1
15	1
16	2
17	4
18	4
19	4
20	4
21	4
22	4
23	3
24	3
25	2
26	2
27	2
28	1
29	1
30	1
31	1
32	1
33	1
34	1
35	1

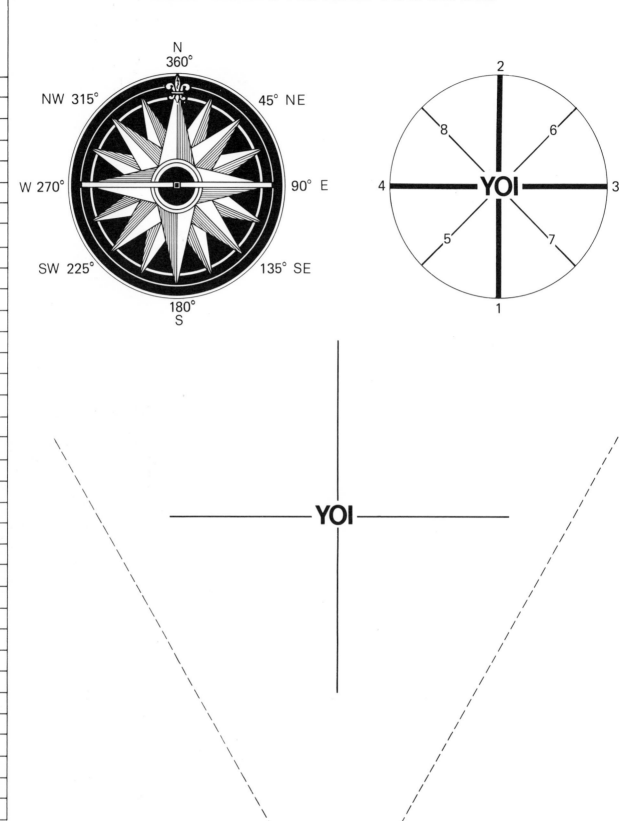

SHIZENTAI

YOI

BOW

SHIZENTAI

YOI

After the "Rei" (Bow) move the right foot into the "Shizentai" position simultaneously crossing the arms in front of the body.

To move into the "Yoi" position, move the right foot across to the left, and both hands to the centre of the body. The left fist should be palm up about three inches above the navel and the right fist vertically over the top of it, with the back of the fist turned out.

MOVEMENT 1

TETTSUI UCHI

YOI

1A

1B

1C

MOVEMENT 1
Tettsui Uchi (Bottom fist strike)

STANCE: Heisoku Dachi (Informal attention stance).

SHIFT 1: Raise the right elbow and turn the head to the right together. Describe a circular movement, brushing the back of the right fist against the left ear. Continue round and stop the right arm when it is straight and the bottom fist in line with the shoulder.

SPEED: Slowly.

BREATHING: In slowly through nose.

DIRECTION: Body 1. Technique 4.

STRIKING

BLOCKING

MOVEMENT 2

PREPARATORY POSITION

TETTSUI UCHI

2A

2B

PREPARATORY POSITION

MOVEMENT 2
Preparatory position

STANCE: Heisoku Dachi
(Informal attention stance).

SHIFT 2: Bring the right arm back
in an arc keeping the head
looking in the same direction as
the fist. Touch the fist in the centre
of the body about 3 inches above
the navel, palm up and turn the left
fist vertically above it.

SPEED: Slowly.

BREATHING: Out through mouth,
slowly.

DIRECTION: Body 1.
Technique 1.

MOVEMENT 3

TETTSUI UCHI

PREPARATORY POSITION

3A

TETTSUI UCHI

MOVEMENT 3
Tettsui Uchi (Bottom fist strike)

STANCE: Heisoku Dachi (Informal attention stance).

SHIFT 3: Follow the identical procedure as in Shift 1 but on this occasion to your left, with your left arm.

SPEED: Slowly.

BREATHING: In through nose slowly.

DIRECTION: Body 1. Technique 3.

STRIKING TO THE HEAD

BLOCKING AN UPPER PUNCHING ATTACK

MOVEMENT 4

AWASA SHUTŌ AGE UKE

4A

4B

AWASE SHUTŌ AGE UKE

SIDE VIEW

MOVEMENT 4
Awase Shutō Age Uke (Double Upper Rising knife hand block)

STANCE: Kiba Dachi (Straddle stance).

SHIFT 4: From movement 3, step across with the left foot into Kiba Dachi, the left hand swinging in a wide arc, whilst the right hand thrusts straight up from the body.

The four fingers of the right hand should cover the fingers of the left.

SPEED: Fast.

BREATHING: Out through mouth quickly.

DIRECTION: 4

BREAKING THE BALANCE BY PULLING THE ARM DOWN

COUNTER PUNCHING WITH A REVERSE PUNCH

TATE SHUTŌ UKE

TATE KEN GYAKU ZUKI

AWASE SHUTŌ AGE UKE

MIDWAY

TATE SHUTŌ UKE
SIDE VIEW

MIDWAY
SIDE VIEW

MOVEMENT 5
Tate Shutō Uke (Vertical knife hand block)

STANCE: Fudō Dachi (Rooted stance).

SHIFT 5: Move the right foot hip width into Fudō Dachi, cup the left ear with the right hand and block Tate Shutō Uke.

SPEED: Slow — half power.

BREATHING: Slow inhalation — slow exhalation.

DIRECTION:

MOVEMENT 6
Tate Ken Gyaku Zuki (Vertical reverse punch)

STANCE: Zenkutsu Dachi (Forward stance).

SHIFT 6: Perform a vertical reverse punch into the palm of the right hand.

SPEED: Fast with focus.

BREATHING: Out through mouth quickly.

DIRECTION:

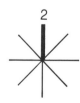

BLOCKING A LUNGE PUNCH

COUNTER ATTACKING WITH A VERTICAL FIST PUNCH

TATE SHUTŌ UKE

TATE KEN GYAKU ZUKI

6

TATE KEN GYAKU ZUKI
FRONT VIEW

MIDWAY
SIDE VIEW

7

TATE SHUTŌ UKE
SIDE VIEW

MIDWAY
SIDEWAY

MOVEMENT 7
Tate Shutō Uke (Vertical knife hand block)

STANCE: Fudō Dachi (Rooted stance)

SHIFT 7: Step forward, left hand over right into a left Fudō Dachi blocking with Tate Shutō Uke.

SPEED: Slow — half power.

BREATHING: Slow inhalation, slow exhalation.

MOVEMENT 8
Tate Ken Gyaku Zuki (Vertical Reverse Punch)

STANCE: Zenkutsu Dachi (Forward stance).

SHIFT 8: Perform a vertical reverse punch into the palm of the left hand.

SPEED: Fast with focus.

BREATHING: Out through mouth quickly.

DIRECTION:

1

BLOCKING A LUNGE PUNCH

2

PULLING THE HEAD ONTO THE ATTACKING FIST

TATE SHUTŌ UKE

TATE ENPI UCHI

TATE KEN GYAKU ZUKI

8

MIDWAY
SIDE VIEW

TATE SHUTŌ UKE

9

MIDWAY
SIDE VIEW

MOVEMENT 9
Tate Shutō Uke (Vertical Knife Hand Block)

STANCE: Fudō Dachi (Rooted stance)

SHIFT 9: Step forward right hand over left into a right Fudō Dachi blocking with Tate Shutō Uke.

SPEED: Slow half power.

BREATHING: Slow inhalation, slow exhalation.

DIRECTION:

MOVEMENT 10
Tate Enpi Uchi (Augmented upper elbow strike)

STANCE: Zenkutsu Dachi (Forward stance).

SHIFT 10: Change into a right forward stance at the same time attack up with a rising elbow strike. The right hand remains

open and presses against the upper left forearm.

SPEED: Fast with focus and Kiai.

BREATHING: Out through mouth quickly.

DIRECTION:

1

BLOCKING A LUNGE PUNCH

2

STRIKING WITH AN UPPER ELBOW STRIKE

HIDARI CHŪDAN SHUTŌ UKE

MIGI CHŪDAN SHUTŌ UKE

KIAI

TATE ENPI UCHI
SIDE VIEW

MIDWAY

**HIDARI CHŪDAN
SHUTŌ UKE**

MIDWAY

**MOVEMENT 11
Hidari Chūdan Shutō Uke (Left
middle knife hand block)**

STANCE: Kōkutsu Dachi (Back
stance).

SHIFT 11: Move the left leg
behind the right and turn 180°
blocking a Chūdan punch with
Shutō Uke.

SPEED: Fast with focus.

BREATHING: In through nose,
out through mouth
fast.

DIRECTION:

1

**MOVEMENT 12
Migi Chūdan Shuto Uke. (Right
middle knife hand block)**

STANCE: Kōkutsu Dachi (Back
stance).

SHIFT 12: Step forward and
perform a right knife hand block in
Kōkutsu Dachi (keep weight back
whilst advancing).

SPEED: Fast with focus.

BREATHING: In through nose,
out through mouth
fast.

DIRECTION:

1

BLOCKING A LUNGE PUNCH

STRIKING WITH A KNIFE HAND STRIKE

BLOCKING A LEFT LUNGE PUNCH

Chinte **43**

KŌSA UKE

GEDAN TETSUI UCHI

12　**MIGI CHŪDAN SHUTŌ UKE**

13A　**JŌDAN MAE GERI**

13B

13　**KŌSA UKE**

14A　**NAIWAN SUKUI NAGE**

14B

MOVEMENT 13
Kosa Uke (Double Block)

STANCE: Zenkutsu Dachi (Forward stance).

SHIFT 13: Keep the hands in the blocking position and kick Jōdan Mae Geri with the left leg putting it back down virtually in the same place it came from but a forward stance, simultaneously blocking Uchi Uke and Gedan Barai.

SPEED: Fast with focus.

BREATHING: Fast in and fast out.

DIRECTION:

1

MOVEMENT 14
Gedan Tettsui Uchi (Lower bottom fist strike)

STANCE: Heisoku Dachi (Informal attention stance).

SHIFT 14: Bring the left foot to the right in Heisoku Dachi and block Naiwan Sukui Nage, continue the blocking arm round in a wide arc-over the head and down striking Gedan Tettsui Uchi.

SPEED: Fast — half power — then full power.

BREATHING: Long inhalation — fast exhalation.

DIRECTION:

1

1　**BLOCKING A PUNCH**

2　**BLOCKING A KICK**

3　**SCOOPING THE LEG**

4　**OPPONENT BECOMES AIRBORNE**

MOROTE ENSHIN HAITŌ BARAI

MOROTE ENSHIN HAITŌ BARAI

14 **GEDAN TETTSUI UCHI**	**15A**	**15B**	**15** **MOROTE ENSHIN HAITŌ BARAI**	**16A**	**16B** **SIDE VIEWS**

MOVEMENT 15
Morote Enshin Haitō Barai (Augmented rotary ridge hand parry)

STANCE: Kiba Dachi (Straddle stance)

SHIFT 15: Swing both hands up and over your head then step back with the right foot into Kiba

Dachi simultaneously blocking with an augmented ridge hand strike.

SPEED: Fast with focus.

BREATHING: In and out fast.

DIRECTION:

1

THROWING — MAXIMUM POWER TWISTS THE ATTACKER VERTICALLY HEAD DOWN ENABLING TETTSUI UCHI TO BE DELIVERED TO THE TEMPLE

BLOCKING A FRONT KICK

MOVEMENT 16
Morote Enshin Haitō Barai (Augmented rotary ridge hand parry

STANCE: Kiba Dachi (Straddle stance).

SHIFT 16: Move both arms across the body to the right, then describe a complete anticlockwise circle blocking on the right hand side with augmented Haitō Barai. Move your stance by sliding to the left when blocking.

SPEED: Fast with focus.

BREATHING: In and out fast.

2

DIRECTION:

RYOWAN UCHI UKE

RYOWAN GAMAE

16
MOROTE ENSHIN HAITŌ BARAI
SIDE VIEW

MIDWAY SIDE VIEW

17
RYOWAN UCHI UKE
SIDE VIEW

18A

18B

18C

BLOCKING A DOUBLE PUNCH . . .

AND BLOCKING A FRONT KICK

MOVEMENT 17
Ryowan Uchi Uke (Double inside forearm block)

STANCE: Kiba Dachi straddle stance.

SHIFT 17: Turn the back of both hands up bringing the right arm over the left and slide both feet to the left at the same time block Ryowan Uchi Uke in Kiba Dachi.

SPEED: Fast with Kime (focus).

BREATHING: In and out fast.

DIRECTION:

MOVEMENT 18
Ryowan Gamae

STANCE: Tsuru Ashi Dachi

SHIFT 18: Move the right foot up to the left and then up behind the left calf simultaneously taking both arms to the sides and then up and over the head crossing down in front of the chest to the Gedan Barai position on either side.

SPEED: Slowly about 4-5 seconds.

BREATHING: Slow inhalation, slow exhalation.

DIRECTION:

IPPON KEN FURI OTOSHI

IPPON KEN GYAKU FURI OTOSHI

RYOWAN GAMAE

MIDWAY

**IPPON KEN FURI
OTOSHI**

MIDWAY

MOVEMENT 19
Ippon Ken Furi Otoshi

STANCE: Zenkutsu Dachi
(forward stance)

SHIFT 19: Step forward into a
right Zenkutsu Dachi whilst
circling the right arm, culminating
in a middle knuckle attack.

SPEED: Fast with focus.

BREATHING: In and out fast.

DIRECTION: 4

MOVEMENT 20
Ippon Ken Gyaku Furi Otoshi

STANCE: Zenkutsu Dachi.

SHIFT 20: Swing your left arm in
a circular fashion over the head
bringing the left fist down on top
of the right one. At this point both
middle knuckles are protruding.

SPEED: Fast with focus.

BREATHING:
In and out fast.

DIRECTION: 4

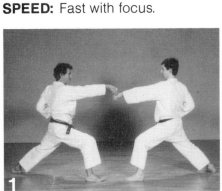

**STRIKING THE ATTACKING FIST WITH A
ONE KNUCKLE FIST ATTACK**

BEING GRABBED

**ATTACKING THE GRABBING HAND WITH A
LEFT MIDDLE KNUCKLE FIST ATTACK**

MIGI UCHI UKE

JŌDAN NIHON NUKITE

20

MIDWAY

21

MIDWAY

IPPON KEN GYAKU FURI OTOSHI

MIGI UCHI UKE

MOVEMENT 21
Migi Uchi Uke (Right inside forearm block)

STANCE: Zenkutsu Dachi.

SHIFT 21: Keeping the left hip pushed forward bring the right fist (two fingers protruding) to a position above the left hip and then twist the hips blocking Chūdan Uchi Uke.

SPEED: Fast with focus.

BREATHING: In and half out.

DIRECTION: 4

MOVEMENT 22
Jōdan Nihon Nukite (Upper two finger spear hand thrust)

STANCE: Zenkutsu Dachi — forward stance.

SHIFT 22: Step forward into a left forward stance and perform a two finger spear hand thrust to the eyes. The attacking hand rises in

very much the same way as in Age Zuki.

SPEED: Fast with focus.

BREATHING: Half out through mouth.

DIRECTION: 4

BLOCKING A LUNGE PUNCH . . .

AND STRIKING TO THE EYES WITH A TWO FINGER SPEAR HAND THRUST

HIDARI UCHI UKE

JŌDAN NIHON NUKITE

22

JŌDAN NIHON NUKITE

MIDWAY

23

HIDARI UCHI UKE

MIDWAY

MOVEMENT 23
Hidari Uchi Uke (Left inside forearm block)

STANCE: Zenkutsu Dachi — forward stance.

SHIFT 23: Pivot on the back foot and turn 180° to block Hidari Uchi Uke with the first two fingers of the left hand extended.

SPEED: Fast with focus.

BREATHING: In and out fast.

DIRECTION: 3

MOVEMENT 24
Jōdan Nihon Nukite (Upper two finger spear hand thrust)

STANCE: Zenkutsu Dachi — forward stance.

SHIFT 24: Step forward into a right Zenkutsu Dachi and attack Jōdan Nihon Nukite. The attacking hand rises as in Age Zuki.

SPEED: Fast with focus.

BREATHING: In and out fast.

DIRECTION: 3

1

BLOCKING A LUNGE PUNCH . . .

2

PULLING BACK AND COUNTER ATTACKING WITH A TWO FINGER SPEAR HAND THRUST TO THE EYES

Chinte   49

CHŪDAN TEISHŌ FURI UCHI

HIDARI TEISHŌ FURI UCHI

JŌDAN NIHON NUKITE

MIDWAY

CHŪDAN TEISHŌ FURI UCHI
FRONT VIEW

MIDWAY
FRONT VIEW

MOVEMENT 25
Chūdan Teishō Furi Uchi
(Middle palm heel strike)

STANCE: Fudō Dachi — Rooted stance.

SHIFT 25: Open the right hand and step 90° to the left into Fudō Dachi performing Teishō Uchi.

SPEED: Fast with focus.

BREATHING: In and out fast.

DIRECTION:

MOVEMENT 26
Hidari Teishō Furi Uchi
(Left palm heel strike)

STANCE: Zenkutsu Dachi — forward stance.

SHIFT 26: Stay on the spot and swing the left hand in a wide arc so the left palm joins the right palm. In doing so, switch to a Zenkutsu Dachi.

SPEED: Fast with focus.

BREATHING: In and out fast (half out).

DIRECTION:

BLOCKING A LUNGE PUNCH WITH A PALM HEEL BLOCK AND . . .

BREAKING THE OFFENDING ARM WITH A PALM HEEL STRIKE

**HAIMEN HASAMI UCHI
(NAKADAKA IPPON KEN)**

**HASAMI UCHI
(NAKADAKA IPPON KEN)**

**HIDARI TEISHŌ
FURI UCHI**
FRONT VIEW

MIDWAY

**HAIMEN HASAMI
UCHI
(NAKADAKA IPPON
KEN)**

MIDWAY

**MOVEMENT 27
Haimen Hasami Uchi —
(Scissors strike) (Nakadaka
Ippon Ken)**

STANCE: Zenkutsu Dachi
(Forward stance).

SHIFT 27: From Teishō Furi Uchi
swing both fists out in a semi circular
manner striking to the ribs with both
middle finger knuckles.

SPEED: Fast with focus.

BREATHING: Out through mouth
(half out)

DIRECTION: Body 2.
Technique 1.

**MOVEMENT 28
Hasami Uchi (Nakadaka Ippon
Ken) (Scissors Strike) (Double
middle finger knuckle attack)**

STANCE: Fudō Dachi (Rooted
stance).

SHIFT 28: Move the rear leg
across behind the body and turn
180° into Fudō Dachi
simultaneously striking to the rib
cage.

SPEED: Fast — focus — Kiai.

BREATHING: In whilst turning,
out whilst attacking.

DIRECTION:

**STRIKING THE RIBS AFTER HAVING BEING
GRASPED FROM BEHIND BY AN
ASSAILANT USING A BEAR HUG**

**TURNING 180° AND REPEATING THE
ATTACK TO THE RIBS**

Chinte   51

TATE SHUTŌ UKE

TATE KEN GYAKU ZUKI

28

HASAMI UCHI
NAKADAKA
IPPON KEN

MIDWAY

29

TATE SHUTŌ UKE

MIDWAY

MOVEMENT 29
Migi Tate Shutō Uke (Right vertical knife hand block)

STANCE: Fudō Dachi (Rooted stance).

SHIFT 29: Step forward with the right leg into Fudō Dachi, blocking with a right Tate Shutō Uke.

SPEED: Slow.

BREATHING: Long inhalation, long exhalation.

DIRECTION:

MOVEMENT 30
Tate Ken Gyaku Zuki (Vertical fist reverse punch)

STANCE: Zenkutsu Dachi (Forward stance)

SHIFT 30: Turn the front knee out, straighten the back leg and thrust the left hip forward as you punch with Tate Zuki into the palm

of the right hand, bringing the body weight forward into Zenkutsu Dachi.

SPEED: Fast with focus.

BREATHING:
Out through mouth.

DIRECTION:

1

BLOCKING A LUNGE PUNCH

2

COUNTER ATTACKING WITH A VERTICAL FIST PUNCH

TATE SHUTŌ UKE

TATE KEN GYAKU ZUKI

30

**TATE KEN GYAKU
ZUKI**

MIDWAY

31

TATE SHUTŌ UKE

MIDWAY

**MOVEMENT 31
Tate Shutō Uke (Vertical knife
hand block)**

STANCE: Fudō Dachi (Rooted
stance).

SHIFT 31: Step forward with the
left leg into Fudō Dachi and
perform a left Tate Shutō Uke.

SPEED: Slow.

BREATHING: Long inhalation,
long exhalation.

DIRECTION:

**MOVEMENT 32
Tate Ken Gyaku Zuki (Vertical
fist reverse punch)**

STANCE: Zenkutsu Dachi
(Forward stance).

SHIFT 32: Punch on the spot with
a vertical fist punch into the palm
of the left hand.

SPEED: Fast with focus.

BREATHING: Out through mouth.

DIRECTION:

1

BLOCKING A LUNGE PUNCH

2

**GRABBING THE HEAD AND
SIMULTANEOUSLY PUNCHING**

TSUTSUMI KEN　JUMP

TSUTSUMI KEN　JUMP

32

TATE KEN GYAKU ZUKI

PULLING FRONT LEG BACK

33

SIDE VIEW
TSUTSUMI KEN

34

TSUTSUMI KEN
SIDE VIEW

MOVEMENT 33
Tsutsumi Ken (Concealed fist)

STANCE: Heisoku Dachi (Informal attention stance).

SHIFT 33: Withdraw the left foot to the right in Heisoku Dachi, bend the arms slightly and jump back about two feet veering a little to your right. Direction 4.

SPEED: Medium speed — no power.

BREATHING: Long inhalation — Breathing out a little on the jump.

DIRECTION:

Facing Direction

1

MOVEMENT 34
Tsutsumi Ken (Concealed fist)

STANCE: Heisoku Dachi (Informal attention stance).

SHIFT 34: Jump back again about two feet once more to your right (Direction 4), at the same time bending your arms a little more.

SPEED: Medium speed — no power.

BREATHING: Breathing out a little on the jump.

DIRECTION:

Facing Direction

1

ATTACKER PREPARES TO ATTACK WITH CHAIN

CHAIN WRAPS AROUND ANKLES

CHAIN IMMOBILIZES DEFENDER. ATTACKER PREPARES TO PUNCH

MOVEMENT 35

TSUTSUMI KEN

JUMP

YAME

TSUTSUMI KEN
SIDE VIEW

YAME

REI (BOW)

MOVEMENT 35
Tsutsumi Ken (Concealed fist)

STANCE: Heisoku Dachi
(Informal attention stance).

SHIFT 35: Jump back again about two feet veering a little to your right (4) bending the arms still further. The arms should now have come from the straight position (Move 32) to the 45° position. Fists level with the mouth.

SPEED: Medium speed — no power.

BREATHING: Out with the remainder of your breath.

DIRECTION:
Facing Direction

1

To shift from Movement 35 into Yame

Move the right leg into Shizentai simultaneously crossing the arms in front of the body in a protective manner — finally, move the right leg up to the left one, bring the hands to the sides, and bow. (Rei)

Kata begins and ends with courtesy — as too, does Karate-Dō.

DEFENDER EVADES PUNCH BY JUMPING BACK AND TO THE RIGHT . . .

AND COUNTER ATTACKS WITH URAKEN UCHI (BACKFIST STRIKE)

CHINTE

REI   SHIZENTAI   YOI   1

6   7   8   9

14   15   16   17

22   23   24   25

30   31   32   33

YAME

REI

*"If you want to know what type
of teacher a person is, you do not
have to study him directly.*

Simply look at his students.

*The character and personality of
the teacher is always reflected
in the students.*

*When I look at my students it is
like looking in the mirror.*

*If they don't look too good — invariably,
something is wrong with me."*

JION

慈

恩

INTRODUCTION

Jion is probably the most traditional Kata practised today in the Shotokan system.

It retains its original name and the character for it has appeared often in Chinese literature since ancient times. Although speculation, it was almost certainly conceived by someone associated with the Jion temple in China, a theory strengthened a great deal by the distinctive salutation at the beginning and end of this Kata.

According to ancient Chinese writings, the Monks of the Jion temple greeted and made themselves known to each other by wrapping the left hand around the right fist.

We know they were taught "Kempo" and were well able to protect themselves without the use of weapons and the salutation would imply, if pressed, they could retaliate, but due to their doctrine, would "rather not". A comparison is readily drawn with the Samurai and his "Sheathed Sword".

Jion utilizes many basic stances, blocks and punches and is truly representative of the Shotokan style.

The system for explaining the Kata is as follows:

On page 62 you will find a schematic diagram of Jion and a picture of the camera used to photograph all the main movements which appear at the top of the following pages. The camera position remains constant and the practitioner begins and ends his Kata facing the camera. If in retreat when his movements are obscured by his back view, we have photographed him from the side or front and this has been clearly marked.

For many years now, throughout Shotokan Karate, students have been taught to move forward, back, to left or right, or to "45°". This applies to basics, Kata and all six forms of basic Kumite.

In this book, to assist in the explanation of Kata, as far as DIRECTION is concerned, I have likened these moves to the points of the compass.

At the top left hand side of page 62 will be found a photograph of a compass showing the four cardinal points of North, South, East and West, together with the four lesser ones of South East, South West, etc., Eight in all — the same eight that cover almost every Shotokan move taught today.

On the top right hand side of the page is a simplified version showing the eight directions. With the practitioner standing in the centre, facing the camera, forward is "One", back is "Two", his left is "Three", and his right "Four".

Once this simple eight point system has been understood, the most advanced Kata can be easily grasped — directionally speaking.

To summarize then — the photograph at the top of the page is the completed move.

The photographs in the centre of the page show the completed moves, possibly at different angles, to aid understanding, plus the midway points. Finally, the practical application is shown at the bottom of the page and a complete summary of Jion appears on Page 88.

There is no substitute for a good teacher and this book is merely intended to compliment that teaching — not replace it.

The following ten elements of Kata, as taught by Kanazawa Sensei, should be borne in mind at all times. Without them, the Kata will be meaningless.

YOI NO KISIN — the spirit of getting ready. The concentration of will and mind against the opponent as a preliminary to the movements of the Kata.

INYO — the active and passive. Always keeping in mind both attack and defence.

CHIKARA NO KYOJAKU — the manner of using strength. The degree of power used for each movement and position in Kata.

WAZA NO KANKYU — the speed of movement. The speed used for each movement and position in Kata.

TAI NO SHINSHUKU — the degree of expansion or contraction. The degree of expansion or contraction of the body in each movement and position in Kata.

KOKYU — breathing. Breath control related to the posture and movement in Kata*.

TYAKUGAN — the aiming points. In Kata you must keep the purpose of the movement in mind.

KIAI — shouting. Shouting at set points in Kata to demonstrate the martial spirit.

KEITAI NO HOJI — correct positioning. Correct positioning in movement and stance.

ZANSHIN — remaining on guard. Remaining on guard at the completion of the Kata (i.e. back to 'Yoi') until told to relax 'Enoy'.

*N.B. KOKYU — Breathing in Kata plays a very important part towards its correct execution. Inhalation takes place via the nose and exhalation through the mouth. In the following Kata, where a "sequence" of techniques occurs, inhalation is immediately followed by exhalation spread over the number of techniques involved, which often are performed in rapid succession.

SCHEMATIC DIAGRAM OF JION AND DIRECTIONAL ANALYSIS

MOVE	DIRECTION
1	1
2	7
3	7
4	7
5	7
6	7
7	5
8	5
9	5
10	5
11	5
12	1
13	1
14	1
15	1
16	1
17	1
18	4
19	4
20	3
21	3
22	2
23	2
24	2
25	2
26	3
27	7
28	4
29	5
30	1
31	1
32	1
33	1
34	1
35	1
36	1
37	4
38	4
39	3
40	3
41	2
42	2
43	2
44	2
45	3
46	4

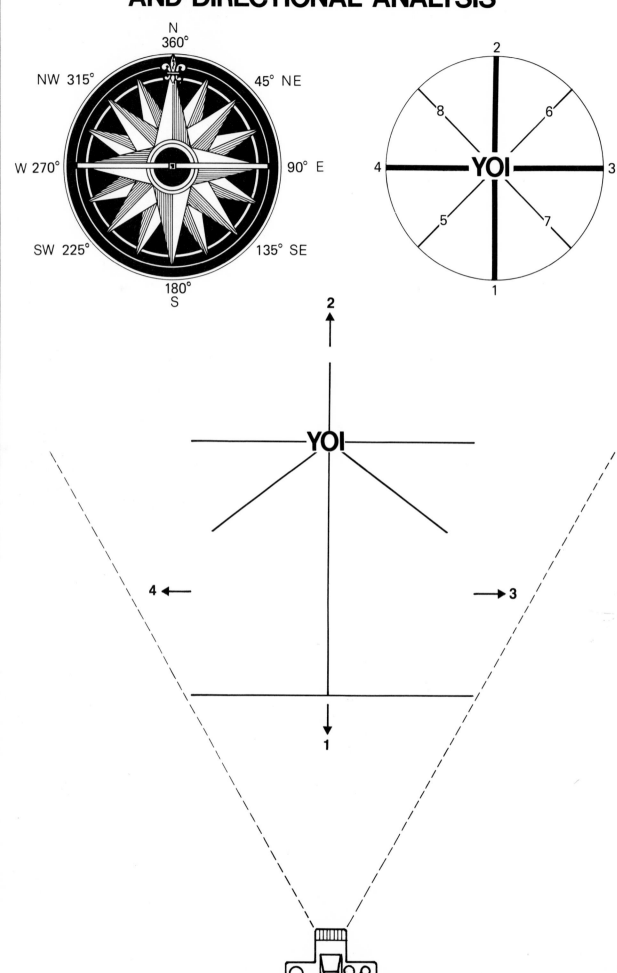

SHIZENTAI

YOI

REI

SHIZENTAI

MIDWAY

YOI

After bowing, move the right foot into "Shizentai". To move into the "Yoi" position, bring the left foot to the right and the right fist into the left hand as illustrated. The forearms should be at 45° and the right fist level with the mouth.

This position is known as 'Jiai No Kamae".

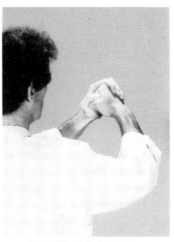

HAND POSITION IN "YOI"

MOVEMENT 1

KŌSA UKE

MOVEMENT 2

KAKIWAKE UKE

YOI

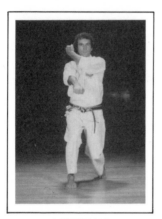

MIDWAY

KŌSA UKE

MIDWAY

MOVEMENT 1:
Kōsa Uke

STANCE: Zenkutsu Dachi.

SHIFT 1: Straighten the right arm in the Gedan position, bring the left fist up to the right ear and step back with the left leg in a forward stance blocking simultaneously Gedan Barai and Uchi Uke.

SPEED: Fast with focus.

BREATHING: In and out fast.

DIRECTION:

MOVEMENT 2:
Kakiwake Uke.

STANCE: Zenkutsu Dachi.

SHIFT 2: Step forward and to 45° (7) into a left forward stance at the same time bringing both fists inverted up in the front of your face and then pull down into the Kakiwake Uke position. The back of the fists finish upwards.

BLOCKING A KICK AND A PUNCH

SPEED: Slowly about 4 seconds.

BREATHING: Long inhalation, long exhalation.

DIRECTION:

BREAKING THE ATTACKERS HOLD

JŌDAN MAE GERI

MIGI CHŪDAN ZUKI

2

KAKIWAKE UKE

MIDWAY

3

JŌDAN MAE GERI

MIDWAY

MOVEMENT 3:
Migi Jōdan Mae Geri

STANCE: Left leg supporting.

SHIFT 3: Do not move the arms whilst performing a right upper front kick.

SPEED: Fast with focus.

BREATHING: ¼ out through mouth.

DIRECTION:

7

MOVEMENT 4:
Migi Chūdan Zuki

STANCE: Zenkutsu Dachi.

SHIFT 4: After snapping the kicking leg back, step forward into a right forward stance executing a right middle punch.

SPEED: Fast with focus.

BREATHING: ¼ out through mouth.

DIRECTION:

7

KICKING TO THE FACE

PUNCHING TO THE BODY

HIDARI GYAKU ZUKI

MIGI CHŪDAN ZUKI

MIGI CHŪDAN ZUKI

MIDWAY

HIDARI GYAKU ZUKI

MIDWAY

**MOVEMENT 5:
Hidari Gyaku Zuki**

STANCE: Zenkutsu Dachi.

SHIFT 5: Perform a left reverse punch on the spot applying the left hip to the full.

SPEED: Fast with focus.

BREATHING: ¼ out through mouth.

DIRECTION:

**MOVEMENT 6:
Migi Chūdan Zuki**

STANCE: Zenkutsu Dachi.

SHIFT 6: Punch with a right middle punch on the spot.

SPEED: Fast with focus.

BREATHING: ¼ out through mouth.

DIRECTION:

COUNTERING WITH A DOUBLE PUNCH TO THE BODY

KAKIWAKE UKE

HIDARI JŌDAN MAE GERI

6

MIGI CHŪDAN ZUKI | MIDWAY

7

KAKIWAKE UKE | MIDWAY

MOVEMENT 7:
Kakiwake Uke

STANCE: Zenkutsu Dachi.

SHIFT 7: Pull the right leg back and out into Direction 5 repeating movement 2 but in right forward stance.

SPEED: Slowly about 4 seconds.

BREATHING: Slow inhalation, slow exhalation.

DIRECTION:

5

MOVEMENT 8:
Hidari Jōdan Mae Geri

STANCE: Right leg supporting.

SHIFT 8: Without moving the arms, perform a left upper front kick.

SPEED: Fast with focus.

BREATHING: ¼ out through mouth.

DIRECTION.

5

BREAKING THE ATTACKERS HOLD

KICKING TO THE FACE

Jion **67**

HIDARI CHŪDAN ZUKI

MIGI CHŪDAN GYAKU ZUKI

HIDARI JŌDAN MAE GERI

MIDWAY

HIDARI CHŪDAN ZUKI

MIDWAY

**MOVEMENT 9:
Hidari Chūdan Zuki**

STANCE: Zenkutsu Dachi.

SHIFT 9: After kicking, snap the leg back, then step forward into a left forward stance and punch with a left middle punch.

SPEED: Fast with focus.

BREATHING: ¼ out through mouth.

DIRECTION:

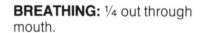

5

**MOVEMENT 10:
Migi Chūdan Gyaku Zuki**

STANCE: Zenkutsu Dachi.

SHIFT 10: Punch on the spot with a right middle reverse punch.

SPEED: Fast with focus.

BREATHING: Out ¼ through mouth.

DIRECTION:

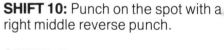

5

COUNTERING WITH "SAMBON ZUKI" TO THE MID SECTION

HIDARI CHŪDAN ZUKI

HIDARI JŌDAN AGE UKE

**MIGI CHŪDAN
GYAKU ZUKI**

MIDWAY

HIDARI CHŪDAN ZUKI

MIDWAY

**MOVEMENT 11:
Hidari Chūdan Zuki**

STANCE: Zenkutsu Dachi.

SHIFT 11: Perform a middle left punch on the spot.

SPEED: Fast with focus.

BREATHING: ¼ out through mouth.

DIRECTION:

**MOVEMENT 12:
Hidari Jōdan Age Uke**

STANCE: Zenkutsu Dachi.

SHIFT 12: Pull the left leg back halfway to the right one at the same time extend the right knife hand up in front of the face and step forward blocking Age Uke taking the left leg forward.

**BLOCKING AN UPPER
PUNCH**

SPEED: Fast with focus.

BREATHING: In and out, fast.

DIRECTION:

**AND ATTACKING WITH AN
UPPER ELBOW STRIKE**

Jion   **69**

MIGI CHŪDAN GYAKU ZUKI

MIGI JŌDAN AGE UKE

12

HIDARI JŌDAN AGE UKE

MIDWAY

13

MIGI CHŪDAN GYAKU ZUKI

MIDWAY

MOVEMENT 13:
Migi Chūdan Gyaku Zuki

STANCE: Zenkutsu Dachi.

SHIFT 13: Perform right middle reverse punch on the spot.

SPEED: Fast with focus.

BREATHING: Out through mouth.

DIRECTION:

MOVEMENT 14:
Migi Jōdan Age Uke

STANCE: Zenkutsu Dachi.

SHIFT 14: Step forward with the right leg into a right forward stance and defend with a right upper rising block.

SPEED: Fast with focus.

BREATHING: In and half out.

DIRECTION:

BLOCKING A LUNGE PUNCH WITH AN UPPER RISING BLOCK

HIDARI CHŪDAN GYAKU ZUKI

HIDARI JŌDAN AGE UKE

MIGI JŌDAN AGE UKE

MIDWAY

HIDARI CHŪDAN GYAKU ZUKI

MIDWAY

MOVEMENT 15:
Hidari Chūdan Gyaku Zuki

STANCE: Zenkutsu Dachi.

SHIFT 15: Execute a left middle reverse punch on the spot.

SPEED: Fast with focus.

BREATHING: Half out through mouth.

DIRECTION:

MOVEMENT 16:
Hidari Jōdan Age Uke

STANCE: Zenkutsu Dachi.

SHIFT 16: Step forward with the left leg into a left forward stance blocking with a left upper rising block.

SPEED: Fast with focus.

BREATHING: In and half out.

DIRECTION:

**COUNTER ATTACKING WITH
A REVERSE PUNCH**

MIGI CHŪDAN OI ZUKI

MANJI UKE

HIDARI JŌDAN AGE UKE

MIDWAY

MIGI CHŪDAN OI ZUKI

MIDWAY

MOVEMENT 17:
Migi Chūdan Oi Zuki

STANCE: Zenkutsu Dachi.

SHIFT 17: Move the right leg forward into a right forward stance performing a Migi (right) middle lunge punch with Kiai.

SPEED: Fast with focus and Kiai.

BREATHING: Remainder of breath out fast.

DIRECTION:

MOVEMENT 18:
Manji Uke

STANCE: Kōkutsu Dachi.

SHIFT 18: Pivot on the front (right) foot and turn 270° to direction 4 executing a double block in back stance.

SPEED: Fast with focus.

BREATHING: In and half out.

DIRECTION:

BLOCKING AN UPPER LUNGE PUNCH

PUSHING THE ATTACKER BACK

DELIVERING A MID SECTION LUNGE PUNCH

MIGI CHŪDAN KAGE ZUKI

MANJI UKE

MANJI UKE

MIGI CHŪDAN KAGE ZUKI (FRONT VIEW)

MIGI CHŪDAN KAGE ZUKI

MIDWAY

MOVEMENT 19:
Migi Chūdan Kage Zuki

STANCE: Kiba Dachi.

SHIFT 19: Slide both feet across to the left (direction 4) into straddle stance. Bring the left fist straight to the left hip and drop the right fist in an arc to punch Kage Zuki.

SPEED: Fast with focus.

BREATHING: Half out through mouth.

DIRECTION:

MOVEMENT 20:
Manji Uke

STANCE: Kōkutsu Dachi.

SHIFT 20: Bring the right fist up to the left ear and pivot on the spot into back stance blocking Manji Uke (Gedan Barai and Jōdan Uchi Uke).

SPEED: Fast with focus.

BREATHING: In and half out.

DIRECTION:

BLOCKING A FRONT KICK WITH A DOWNWARD BLOCK

COUNTER ATTACKING WITH A HOOK PUNCH

HIDARI CHŪDAN KAGE ZUKI

HIDARI GEDAN BARAI

MANJI UKE

**HIDARI CHŪDAN
KAGE ZUKI**

**HIDARI CHŪDAN
KAGE ZUKE**
FRONT VIEW

MIDWAY

**MOVEMENT 21:
Hidari Chūdan Kage Zuki**

STANCE: Kiba Dachi.

SHIFT 21: Bring the right fist straight to the right hip, drop the left fist in an arc punching Kage Zuki as the body slides to the right (direction 3) into Kiba Dachi.

SPEED: Fast with focus.

BREATHING: Out half breath through mouth.

DIRECTION:

**MOVEMENT 22:
Hidari Gedan Barai.**

STANCE: Zenkutsu Dachi.

SHIFT 22: Bring the left foot almost up to the right then forward (direction 2) into a left forward stance. At the same time block with a left Gedan Barai.

SPEED: Fast with focus.

BREATHING: In and out.

DIRECTION:

**BLOCKING A FRONT KICK
WITH A DOWNWARD BLOCK**

MIGI TEISHŌ UCHI

HIDARI TEISHŌ UCHI

HIDARI GEDAN BARAI
FRONT VIEW

22

MIDWAY

MIGI TEISHŌ UCHI
FRONT VIEW

23

MIDWAY

MOVEMENT 23:
Migi Teishō Uchi

STANCE: Kiba Dachi.

SHIFT 23: Step forward (direction 2) with the right foot into straddle stance. The right hand opens and turns palm down from its inverted fist position at the commencement of this technique and strikes with palm heel strike to the mid section.

SPEED: Fast with focus.

BREATHING: In and out.

DIRECTION:

2

MOVEMENT 24:
Hidari Teishō Uchi

STANCE: Kiba Dachi.

SHIFT 24: Same as 23 but opposite side.

SPEED: Fast with focus.

BREATHING: In and out.

DIRECTION:

2

ATTACKING THE MID SECTION WITH A PALM HEEL STRIKE

MIGI TEISHŌ UCHI

MANJI UKE

HIDARI TEISHŌ UCHI
FRONT VIEW

MIDWAY

MIGI TEISHŌ UCHI
FRONT VIEW

MIDWAY

MOVEMENT 25:
Migi Teishō Uchi

STANCE: Kiba Dachi.

SHIFT 25: Identical to movement 23.

SPEED: Fast with focus.

BREATHING: In and out.

DIRECTION:

MOVEMENT 26:
Manji Uke.

STANCE: Kōkutsu Dachi.

SHIFT 26: Pivot on the right foot and turn the body 90° (direction 3) into back stance executing a double block. The head actually turns 270°.

SPEED: Fast with focus.

BREATHING: In and out.

DIRECTION:

USING AN AUGMENTED
UPPER BLOCK TO COUNTER
AN UPPER LUNGE PUNCH

JŌDAN MOROTE UKE

MANJI UKE

MANJI UKE

MIDWAY

JŌDAN MOROTE UKE

MIDWAY

MOVEMENT 27:
Jōdan Morote Uke

STANCE: Heisoku Dachi.

SHIFT 27: Swing the left fist round to the right hip, move the right foot sharply to the left and block Jōdan Morote Uke. The arms and leg move together.

SPEED: Fast with focus.

BREATHING: In and out.

DIRECTION:

Body direction 1 — technique actually 45°.

MOVEMENT 28:
Manji Uke

STANCE: Kōkutsu Dachi.

SHIFT 28: Step out with the right leg direction 4 into back stance performing a double block of Gedan Barai and Jōdan Uchi Uke.

SPEED: Fast with focus.

BREATHING: In and out.

**STRIKING WITH A
BACK FIST STRIKE**

JŌDAN MOROTE UKE

RYOWAN GAMAE

MANJI UKE   MIDWAY

JŌDAN MOROTE UKE   MIDWAY

MOVEMENT 29:
Jōdan Morote Uke

STANCE: Heisoku Dachi.

SHIFT 29: Bring the right fist to the left hip and at the same time, bring the left foot to the right one as you block Jōdan Morote Uke.

SPEED: Fast with focus.

BREATHING: In and out.

DIRECTION:

1 (body) technique actually 45°

MOVEMENT 30:
Ryowan Gamae

STANCE: Heisoku Dachi.

SHIFT 30: The stance remains the same. The arms cross over the head and down to their respective sides.

SPEED: Slowly, about 4 seconds.

BREATHING: Long inhalation, long exhalation.

DIRECTION:

USING THE UPPER AUGMENTED BLOCK AS A STRIKE TO THE FACE.

READY POSITION

GEDAN JŪJI UKE

RYOWAN GEDAN KAKIWAKE

RYOWAN GAMAE 30

MIDWAY

GEDAN JUJI UKE 31

MIDWAY

MOVEMENT 31:
Gedan Jūji Uke

STANCE: Kosa Dachi.

SHIFT 31: Bring both fists to the waist and raise the right knee. Step forward with the right leg bringing the left close behind it, bending the knees and blocking the attacking front kick with an X block.

SPEED: Fast with focus.

BREATHING: In and half out.

DIRECTION:

1

MOVEMENT 32:
Ryowan Gedan Kakiwake

STANCE: Zenkutsu Dachi.

SHIFT 32: Step back with the left leg bringing both arms down and back into the Gedan Barai position.

SPEED: Fast with focus.

BREATHING: Half out fast.

DIRECTION:

1

DEFENDING AGAINST A FRONT KICK

STEPPING BACK AND PARRYING THE ATTACKING LEG

SŌWAN UCHI UKE

JŌDAN JŪJI UKE

**RYOWAN
GEDAN KAKIWAKE**

MIDWAY

SŌWAN UCHI UKE

MIDWAY

MOVEMENT 33:
Sōwan Uchi Uke

STANCE: Zenkutsu Dachi.

SHIFT 33: Step forward into a left forward stance bringing the left arm over the right and block with a double inside forearm block.

SPEED: Fast with focus.

BREATHING: Fast in and out (about 1/3).

DIRECTION:

MOVEMENT 34:
Jōdan Jūji Uke

STANCE: Zenkutsu Dachi.

SHIFT 34: Step with the right foot into a right forward stance simultaneously thrusting both arms up (without pulling back to the waist) to block with an upper X block. The right arm is in front of the left.

SPEED: Fast with focus.

BREATHING: Out (about 1/3).

DIRECTION:

BLOCKING

BLOCKING

MIGI URA ZUKI HIDARI AGE UKE

MIGI JŌDAN URA ZUKI

JŌDAN JŪJI UKE

MIDWAY

**MIGI URA ZUKI
HIDARI AGE UKE**

**MIGI JŌDAN
NAGASHI UKE**

MOVEMENT 35:
Migi Ura Zuki

STANCE: Zenkutsu Dachi.

SHIFT 35: Thrust the right fist forward and attack with an upper close punch at the same time, twist the left arm up into left upper rising block. Thrust the left hip forward.

SPEED: Fast with focus.

BREATHING: Out (about 1/3).

DIRECTION:

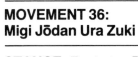

MOVEMENT 36:
Migi Jōdan Ura Zuki

STANCE: Zenkutsu Dachi.

SHIFT 36: Pull the right fist back behind the right ear at the same time thrust the left arm forward.

Bring the right fist forward and strike with an upper close punch bringing the left wrist underneath the right elbow.

SPEED: Fast with focus.

BREATHING: In through nose out through mouth.

DIRECTION:

BLOCKING AND STRIKING

BLOCKING AND PUNCHING

STRIKING

HIDARI CHŪDAN UCHI UKE

MIGI CHŪDAN OI ZUKI

MIGI JŌDAN URA ZUKI

MIDWAY

HIDARI CHŪDAN UCHI UKE

MIDWAY

MOVEMENT 37:
Hidari Chūdan Uchi Uke

STANCE: Zenkutsu Dachi.

SHIFT 37: Pivot on the right foot and turn 270° blocking with an inside forearm block in forward stance.

SPEED: Fast with focus.

BREATHING: In and out (half out).

DIRECTION: 4

MOVEMENT 38:
Migi Chūdan Oi Zuki.

STANCE: Zenkutsu Dachi.

SHIFT 38: Step forward with the right foot (direction 4) into a right forward stance punching with a right lunge punch.

SPEED: Fast with focus.

BREATHING: Out (half out).

DIRECTION: 4

BLOCKING A LUNGE PUNCH

MIGI CHŪDAN UCHI UKE

HIDARI CHŪDAN OI ZUKI

MIGI CHŪDAN OI ZUKI

MIDWAY

MIGI CHŪDAN UCHI UKE

MIDWAY

MOVEMENT 39:
Migi Chūdan Uchi Uke.

STANCE: Zenkutsu Dachi.

SHIFT 39: Move the right foot back and hip width behind the left foot and turn 180° into a right forward stance blocking with an inside forearm block.

SPEED: Fast with focus.

BREATHING: In and half out through mouth.

DIRECTION: 3

MOVEMENT 40:
Hidari Chūdan Oi Zuki.

STANCE: Zenkutsu Dachi.

SHIFT 40: Step forward (Direction 3) with the left foot into a left forward stance punching with a left Chūdan lunge punch.

SPEED: Fast with Kime.

BREATHING: Half out through mouth.

DIRECTION:  3

**PUSHING THE ATTACKER
BACK**

**COUNTER ATTACKING
WITH A LUNGE PUNCH**

HIDARI GEDAN BARAI

MIGI OTOSHI UKE DŌJI FUMIKOMI

HIDARI CHŪDAN OI ZUKI

MIDWAY

HIDARI GEDAN BARAI

MIDWAY

MOVEMENT 41: Hidari Gedan Barai

STANCE: Zenkutsu Dachi.

SHIFT 41: Pull the left foot back and to the left (direction 2) 90° twist and block downward block with the left arm.

SPEED: Fast with focus.

BREATHING: In and out.

DIRECTION:

MOVEMENT 42: Migi Otoshi Uke Dōji Fumikomi.

STANCE: Kiba Dachi.

SHIFT 42: Swing the right leg up in an arc and the right arm up over the head. Come down into straddle stance blocking with a right downward pressing block and attacking the instep with a right stamping kick.

SPEED: Fast with focus.

BREATHING: In and out.

DIRECTION:

PREPARING TO BLOCK

BLOCKING THE ARM ATTACKING THE INSTEP

HIDARI OTOSHI UKE DŌJI FUMIKOMI   **MIGI OTOSHI UKE DŌJI FUMIKOMI**

MIGI OTOSHI UKE
FRONT VIEW   MIDWAY

HIDARI OTOSHI UKE
FRONT VIEW   MIDWAY

**Movement 43:
Hidari Otoshi Uke
Dōji Fumikomi.**

STANCE: Kiba Dachi.

SHIFT 43: Repeat shift 42 but on the opposite side.

SPEED: Fast with focus.

BREATHING: In and out.

DIRECTION:

2

**MOVEMENT 44:
Migi Otoshi Uke
Dōji Fumikomi**

STANCE: Kiba Dachi.

SHIFT 44: Repeat Shift 42. Shift 44 is identical.

SPEED: Fast with focus.

BREATHING: In and out.

DIRECTION:

2

**GRASPING THE PUNCHING ARM AND ATTACKING THE BACK OR
NECK WITH A DOWNWARD BOTTOM FIST STRIKE**

HIDARI YUMI ZUKI

MIGI YUMI ZUKI

MIGI OTOSHI UKE
FRONT VIEW

JŌDAN TSUKAMI UKE

HIDARI YUMI ZUKI

MIDWAY
JŌDAN TSUKAMI UKE

MOVEMENT 45:
Hidari Yumi Zuki

STANCE: Kiba Dachi.

SHIFT 45: Pivot on the right foot turning 270° bringing the right hand around in front of the face blocking "Jodan Tsukami Uke". Slide to the side into Kiba Dachi pulling the right arm back to the chest and punching with the left "Yumi Zuki".

SPEED: Slow — about 5 seconds.

BREATHING: Slow inhalation, slow exhalation.

DIRECTION:

MOVEMENT 46:
Migi Yumi Zuki.

STANCE: Kiba Dachi.

SHIFT 46: Bring the left hand around in front of the face and the right fist to the right hip. With the left hand block with "Tsukami Uke", then pull the left arm back to the chest and punch with Migi Yumi Zuki to the mid section. At the same time, slide both feet across to the right, direction 4 and execute a long slow Kiai. The Kiai should last about 3 seconds.

SPEED: Slow about 5 seconds.

BREATHING: Slow inhalation — slow exhalation.

DIRECTION:

CATCHING THE PUNCHING ARM AND PULLING THE ATTACKER ONTO A THRUSTING PUNCH

YAME

SHIZENTAI

KIAI

MIGI YUMI ZUKI

MIDWAY

YAME

SHIZENTAI

To finish, go into the "Yame" position of "Jiai No Kamae" by pulling the right leg back to the left and the right fist into the palm of the left hand, breathing in slowly as you do so.

To revert to the "Shizentai" position move the left foot to the left (Direction 3) about hip width and cross the arms in front of the body.

To bow ("Rei") bring the right foot to the left and bow.

REI

JION

REI

YOI

KIAI (17)

KIAI (46)

YAME

REI

MIGI YUMI ZUKI

JITTE

十手

INTRODUCTION

The name Jitte, or Jutte, as it is sometimes referred to, implies that once this kata has been mastered, one is as effective as ten men. Its somewhat heavy movements indicate that it belongs to the Shorei School and many of its techniques are strong and bold.

In the Shotokan style, Jitte is an intermediate Kata having twenty-six movements and is mainly practised as a defence against the "Bo".

The absence of kicks points to its origin, for it was an essential part of training at the Tomari School of "Te" in the Seventeenth Century.

The system for explaining the Kata is as follows:

On page 94 you will find a schematic diagram of Jitte and a picture of the camera used to photograph all the main movements which appear at the top of the following pages. The camera position remains constant and the practitioner begins and ends his Kata facing the camera. If in retreat when his movements are obscured by his back view, we have photographed him from the side or front and this has been clearly marked.

For many years now, throughout Shotokan Karate, students have been taught to move forward, back, to left or right, or to "45°". This applies to basics, Kata and all six forms of basic Kumite.

In this book, to assist in the explanation of Kata, as far as DIRECTION is concerned, I have likened these moves to the points of the compass.

At the top left hand side of page 94 will be found a photograph of a compass showing the four cardinal points of North, South, East and West, together with the four lesser ones of South East, South West, etc., eight in all — the same eight that cover almost every Shotokan move taught today.

On the top right hand side of the page is a simplified version showing the eight directions. With the practitioner standing in the centre, facing the camera, forward is "One", back is "Two", his left is "Three", and his right "Four".

Once this simple eight point system has been understood, the most advanced Kata can be easily understood — directionally speaking.

To summarize then — the photograph at the top of the page is the completed move.

The photographs in the centre of the page show the completed moves, possibly at different angles to aid understanding, plus the midway points. Finally, the practical application is shown at the bottom of the page and a complete summary of Jitte appears on Page 112.

There is no substitute for a good teacher and this book is merely intended to complement that teaching — not replace it.

The following ten elements of Kata, as taught by Kanazawa Sensei, should be borne in mind at all times. Without them, the Kata will be meaningless.

YOI NO KISIN — the spirit of getting ready. The concentration of will and mind against the opponent as a preliminary to the movements of the Kata.

INYO — the active and passive. Always keeping in mind both attack and defence.

CHIKARA NO KYOJAKU — the manner of using strength. The degree of power used for each movement and position in Kata.

WAZA NO KANKYU — the speed of movement. The speed used for each movement and position in Kata.

TAI NO SHINSHUKU — the degree of expansion or contraction. The degree of expansion or contraction of the body in each movement and position in Kata.

KOKYU — breathing. Breath control related to the posture and movement in Kata*.

TYAKUGAN — the aiming points. In Kata you must keep the purpose of the movement in mind.

KIAI — shouting. Shouting at set points in Kata to demonstrate the martial spirit.

KEITAI NO HOJI — correct positioning. Correct positioning in movement and stance.

ZANSHIN — remaining on guard. Remaining on guard at the completion of the Kata (i.e. back to 'Yoi') until told to relax 'Enoy'.

*N.B. KOKYU — Breathing in Kata plays a very important part towards its correct execution. Inhalation takes place via the nose and exhalation through the mouth. In the following Kata, where a "sequence" of techniques occurs, inhalation is immediately followed by exhalation spread over the number of techniques involved, which often are performed in rapid succession.

十手

"YAMA UKE—DŌJI FUMIKOMI"

SCHEMATIC DIAGRAM OF JITTE AND DIRECTIONAL ANALYSIS

MOVE	DIRECTION
1	1
2	7
3	4
4	4
5	1
6	1
7	1
8	2
9	2
10	2
11	1
12	1
13	1
14	4
15	2
16	2
17	2
18	2
19	2
20	2
21	3
22	4
23	1
24	1
25	2
26	2

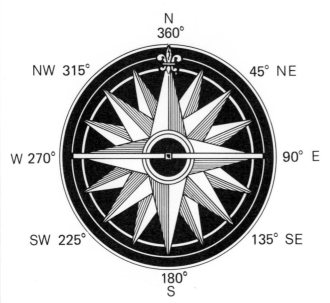

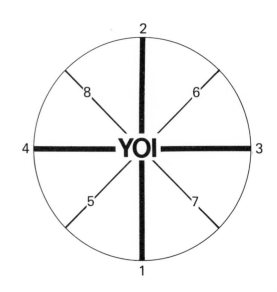

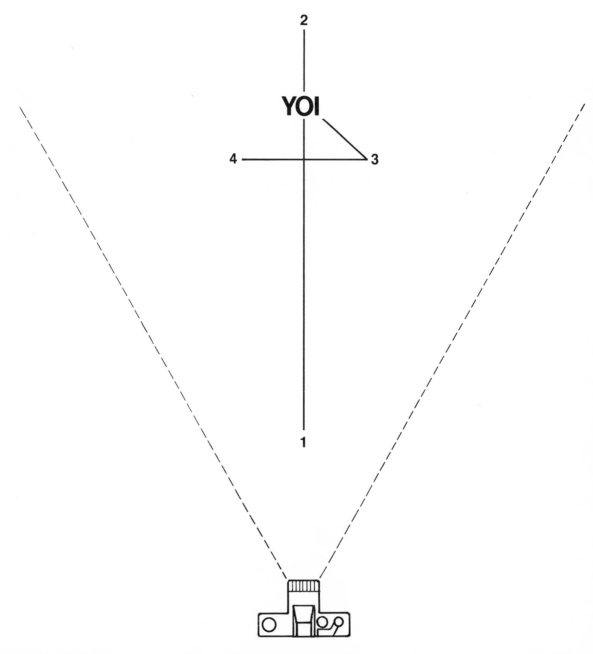

SHIZENTAI

YOI

REI

SHIZENTAI

MIDWAY

**YOI
JIAI NO KAMAE**

After bowing in Heisoku Dachi, move the right foot to the right, about hip width, assuming the Shizentai Position. To go into the "Yoi" position of "Jiai No Kamae" bring the left foot slowly to the right one simultaneously wrapping the left hand around the right fist, keeping the hands in line with the mouth.

MIGI TEKUBI KAKE UKE

YOI
JIAI NO KAMAE

MIDWAY

MIDWAY

MIGI TEKUBI
KAKE UKE
1

MOVEMENT 1
Migi Tekubi Kake Uke

STANCE: Zenkutsu Dachi.

SHIFT 1: This technique involves a Mawashi (circular) Teishō (palm) block and finally concludes with a back hand block against a Jōdan punch. The most common application consists of a right Chūdan Teishō Uke followed by a left Chūdan Teishō Uke, culminating with Migi Tekubi Kake Uke.

SPEED: Slowly — about 5 seconds.

BREATHING: Slow inhalation — slow exhalation.

DIRECTION:

APPLICATIONS FOR THIS MOVEMENT ARE ON PAGE 115

TEISHŌ MOROTE UKE

HIDARI HAITŌ UKE

MIDWAY   MIDWAY   **TEISHŌ MOROTE UKE**   **HIDARI HAITŌ UKE**
                                       2   **3**

MOVEMENT 2
Teishō Morote Uke

STANCE: Zenkutsu Dachi.

SHIFT 2: Move the left foot near to the right and then out 45° (direction 7) into a left forward stance at the same time blocking a middle lunge punch with Teishō Uke.

SPEED: Slowly about 3-4 seconds.

BREATHING: Slow inhalation — slow exhalation.

DIRECTION:

MOVEMENT 3
Hidari Haitō Uke

STANCE: Zenkutsu Dachi.

SHIFT 3: Turn the head sharply to the right (direction 4) and execute a left ridge hand block, touching the right upper arm.

SPEED: Fast with focus.

BLOCKING A LUNGE PUNCH WITH A RIDGE HAND BLOCK

BREATHING: Out through mouth.

DIRECTION:

Stance remains in Direction 7.

GRABBING AND COUNTER ATTACKING WITH A RIDGE HAND STRIKE   97

MIGI HAITŌ UCHI

MIGI TEISHŌ UCHI

HIDARI HAITŌ UKE
3

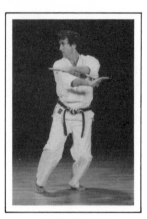

MIDWAY

MIGI HAITŌ UCHI
4

MIDWAY

MOVEMENT 4
Migi Haitō Uchi

STANCE: Kiba Dachi.

SHIFT 4: Move the right foot in an arc and out into Kiba Dachi (straddle stance) in direction 4 performing a right ridge hand strike.

SPEED: Fast with focus.

BREATHING: In and out fast.

DIRECTION:

MOVEMENT 5
Migi Teishō Uchi

STANCE: Kiba Dachi.

SHIFT 5: Move the left foot halfway to the right and step forward with the right foot into Kiba Dachi (straddle stance) striking with the right palm heel.

SPEED: Fast with focus.

BREATHING: In through nose and partially out through mouth.

DIRECTION:

MOVING IN AND ATTACKING WITH A RIGHT MIDDLE PALM HEEL STRIKE

HIDARI TEISHŌ UCHI

MIGI TEISHŌ UCHI

MIGI TEISHŌ UCHI
5

MIDWAY

HIDARI TEISHŌ UCHI
6

MIDWAY

MOVEMENT 6
Hidari Teishō Uchi

STANCE: Kiba Dachi.

SHIFT 6: Move the left foot past the right one and forward into straddle stance performing a left palm heel strike.

SPEED: Fast with focus.

BREATHING: Partially out through mouth.

DIRECTION:

1

MOVEMENT 7
Migi Teishō Uchi

STANCE: Kiba Dachi.

SHIFT 7: From movement 6, step forward with the right foot into straddle stance executing a right palm heel strike.

SPEED: Fast with focus.

BREATHING: Remainder of breath out.

DIRECTION:

1

BLOCKING A LUNGE PUNCH   **STRIKING—PALM HEEL STRIKE**
TEISHŌ USED AS DEFENSE OR ATTACK

JŌDAN JŪJI UKE

RYOWAN GEDAN KAKIWAKE

MIGI TEISHŌ UCHI
7

MIDWAY

JŌDAN JŪJI UKE
8

MIDWAY

MOVEMENT 8
Jōdan Jūji Uke

STANCE: Kōsa Dachi.

SHIFT 8: Step over the left foot with the right one into Kōsa Dachi blocking with an upper X block. The whole body rises up during this technique.

SPEED: Fast with focus.

BREATHING: In through nose.

DIRECTION:
Head facing Direction 3.

MOVEMENT 9
Ryowan Gedan Kakiwake

STANCE: Kiba Dachi.

SHIFT 9: Step direction 2 with the left foot into straddle stance bringing both arms down to the sides in the Gedan Barai position to complete Ryowan Gedan Kakiwake.

SPEED: Fast with Focus.

BREATHING:
Out through mouth.

DIRECTION:
Head facing Direction 3.

BLOCKING A LUNGE PUNCH
WITH AN UPPER X BLOCK

SIDE STEPPING AND
BREAKING THE BALANCE

COUNTER ATTACKING
WITH A REVERSE PUNCH

YAMA KAKIWAKE

YAMA UKE-DŌJI FUMIKOMI

**RYOWAN GEDAN
KAKIWAKE
9**

MIDWAY

**YAMA KAKIWAKE
10**

MIDWAY

MOVEMENT 10
Yama Kakiwake

STANCE: Kiba Dachi.

SHIFT 10: Move the right foot to the left and then the left foot out into Kiba Dachi simultaneously crossing the arms left over right and perform Yama Kakiwake.

SPEED:

BREATHING: In and out fast.

DIRECTION:

Head facing Direction 3.

MOVEMENT 11
Yama Uke Dōji Fumikomi

STANCE: Kiba Dachi.

SHIFT 11: Turn the head sharply to the right and keeping the left leg bent, swing it in an arc and bring it down into Kiba Dachi simultaneously blocking with a U block. Whilst the left leg is moving the left arm should be kept as far back as possible.

SPEED: Fast with focus.

BREATHING: In through nose, out through mouth.

DIRECTION:

**YAMA UKE BLOCKING
A LUNGE PUNCH**

**YAMA UKE BLOCKING
A "BO" ATTACK**

YAMA UKE-DŌJI FUMIKOMI

YAMA UKE-DŌJI FUMIKOMI

**YAMA UKE
DŌJI FUMIKOMI
11**

MIDWAY

**YAMA UKE
DŌJI FUMIKOMI
12**

MIDWAY

**MOVEMENT 12
Yama Uke Dōji Fumikomi**

STANCE: Kiba Dachi.

SHIFT 12: Repeat movement 11, but on the right side. N.B. As the right foot touches the floor in Kiba Dachi, in practice, it performs a stamping kick to the opponent's instep.

SPEED: Fast with focus.

BREATHING: In through nose, out through mouth.

DIRECTION:

**MOVEMENT 13
Yama Uke Dōji Fumikomi**

STANCE: Kiba Dachi.

SHIFT 13: Repeat movement 11 but with Kiai.

SPEED: Fast with focus and "Kiai".

BREATHING:
In and out fast.

DIRECTION:

BLOCKING THE "BO"

GRABBING, TWISTING AND BREAKING THE BALANCE

RYOWAN GAMAE

MIGI JŌDAN SHUTŌ UKE

**YAMA UKE
DŌJI FUMIKOMI
13**

MIDWAY

**RYOWAN GAMAE
14**

MIDWAY

**MOVEMENT 14
Ryowan Gamae**

STANCE: Shizentai.

SHIFT 14: Tightening the stomach muscles, pull both feet inwards into Shizentai, crossing the arms over the head (right inside left) and down to their respective sides.

SPEED: Slowly about 3 seconds.

BREATHING: In quickly and slowly out through mouth.

DIRECTION:

4 ——

**MOVEMENT 15
Migi Jōdan Shutō Uke**

STANCE: Zenkutsu Dachi.

SHIFT 15: Cross the arms in front of the chest (hands palms down) and move the right foot onto a forward stance blocking at the same time with an upper knife hand block.

SPEED: Fast with focus.

BREATHING: In and out fast.

DIRECTION:

2

**THROWING, FOLLOWED BY
A COUNTER ATTACK**

APPLICATIONS FOR MOVEMENTS 15-20 ARE ON PAGE 116

MOROTE JO UKE

MOROTE JO DORI

MIGI JŌDAN SHUTŌ UKE
15
FRONT

MIDWAY
FRONT

MOROTE JO UKE
16
FRONT

MIDWAY
MOROTE KOKŌ DORI
FRONT

MOVEMENT 16
Morote Jo Uke

MOVEMENT 17
Morote Jo Dori

STANCE: Zenkutsu Dachi.

SHIFT 16: Lower the right hand to a low Chūdan level simultaneously thrusting the left hand forward at Jōdan level. The hands are now in line vertically and blocking a Bo attack (stick).

SPEED: Fast.

BREATHING: Breathing out.

DIRECTION:

STANCE: Sagi Ashi Dachi.

SHIFT 17: Twist both hands 180° clockwise into Morote Kokō Dori. Keeping them at the same distance apart, revolve them anticlockwise until the left hand is directly under the right one. At this point the palms are facing downwards. Now move the left foot up to the right knee and pull the arms to the side of the body as illustrated, palms facing down.

SPEED: Slowly about 3-4 seconds. Half power.

BREATHING: Slow inhalation.

MIDWAY
FRONT

DIRECTION:

MOROTE JO TSUKI DACHI

MOROTE JO DORI

MOROTE JO DORI
17
FRONT VIEW

MIDWAY
FRONT VIEW

MOROTE JO TSUKI
DACHI
18
FRONT VIEW

MOROTE KOKŌ
DORI
FRONT VIEW

MOVEMENT 18
Morote Jo Tsuki Dachi

STANCE: Zenkutsu Dachi.

SHIFT 18: Step forward (Direction 2) into a left forward stance thrusting both hands forward, the left at Chūdan and the right at Jōdan. Both hands are palm down, in the Tigers Mouth position and are in line vertically.

SPEED: Fast with focus.

BREATHING: Out through mouth.

DIRECTION:

MOVEMENT 19
Morote Jo Dori

STANCE: Sagi Ashi Dachi.

SHIFT 19: Repeat movement 17 but on the opposite side.

SPEED: Slowly, about 3-4 seconds, half power.

BREATHING: Slow inhalation.

DIRECTION:

MIDWAY
FRONT

MOROTE JO TSUKI DACHI

MANJI UKE

MOROTE JO DORI
19
FRONT VIEW

MOROTE JO
TSUKI DACHI
20
FRONT VIEW

MIDWAY

MANJI UKE
21

MOVEMENT 20
Morote Jo Tsuki Dachi

STANCE: Zenkutsu Dachi.

SHIFT 20: Step forward (direction 2) into a right forward stance thrusting both hands forward, the right at Chūdan, the left at Jōdan. Both hands are palm down, in the Tigers Mouth position and are in line vertically.

SPEED: Fast with focus.

BREATHING:
Out through mouth.

DIRECTION:

MOVEMENT 21
Manji Uke

STANCE: Kokutsu Dachi.

SHIFT 21: Move the left foot up to the right one and out to direction 3 (turning 270°) twisting the body and hips into a left back stance blocking Manji Uke (Gedan Barai, Jōdan Uchi Uke).

BLOCKING A FRONT KICK

SPEED: Fast with focus.

BREATHING: In and out fast.

DIRECTION:

COUNTERING WITH A
KNIFE HAND STRIKE

MANJI UKE

HIDARI JŌDAN AGE UKE

MIDWAY

MANJI UKE
22

MIDWAY

HIDARI JŌDAN
AGE UKE
23

MOVEMENT 22
Manji Uke

STANCE: Kōkutsu Dachi.

SHIFT 22: Move the right fist behind the left ear, twist the body and hips into a right back stance and block Manji Uke.

SPEED: Fast with focus.

BREATHING: In and out fast.

DIRECTION:

MOVEMENT 23
Hidari Jōdan Age Uke

STANCE: Zenkutsu Dachi.

SHIFT 23: Move the left foot halfway to the right and forward (direction 1) into a left forward stance. In so doing, extend the right arm upwards and perform a left upper rising block.

SPEED: Fast with focus.

BREATHING: In and out partially fast.

DIRECTION:

APPLICATIONS FOR
MOVEMENT 23 ARE ON PAGE 117

MIGI JŌDAN AGE UKE

HIDARI JŌDAN AGE UKE

MIDWAY

MIGI JŌDAN AGE UKE
24

MIDWAY

HIDARI JŌDAN AGE UKE
25

MOVEMENT 24
Migi Jōdan Age Uke

STANCE: Zenkutsu Dachi.

SHIFT 24: Step forward and perform a right upper rising block.

SPEED: Fast with focus.

BREATHING: Out partially through mouth.

DIRECTION:

MOVEMENT 25
Hidari Jōdan Age Uke

STANCE: Zenkutsu Dachi.

SHIFT 25: Turn 180° (direction 2) and execute a left upper rising block.

SPEED: Fast with focus.

BREATHING: Out partially through mouth.

DIRECTION:

BLOCKING AN UPPER LUNGE PUNCH AND COUNTERING WITH A REVERSE UPPER ELBOW STRIKE

MIGI JŌDAN AGE UKE

YAME

MIDWAY

MIGI JŌDAN AGE UKE 26

MIDWAY

YAME JIAI NO KAMAE

**MOVEMENT 26
Migi Jōdan Age Uke**

STANCE: Zenkutsu Dachi.

SHIFT 26: Step forward, thrusting the hips to gain a little more distance, and perform a right upper rising block with Kiai.

SPEED: Fast with focus and Kiai.

BREATHING: Remainder of breath out through mouth.

DIRECTION:

To resume the Yoi position bring the left foot up to the right one and pivot 180°, wrapping the left hand around the right fist.

SIMULTANEOUSLY BLOCKING AND ATTACKING THE CHIN WITH A HAMMER FIST STRIKE

SHIZENTAI

REI

YAME

SHIZENTAI

HEISOKU DACHI

REI

Move the left foot to the left about hip width and cross the arms in front of the body into the Shizentai position.

In order to bow and complete the Kata, move the right foot to the left in Heisoku Dachi, bring the hands to the sides of the body — and Rei.

Kata, like Karate-Do, begins and ends with courtesy . . .

"MOROTE JO DORI"
"SAGI ASHI DACHI"

JITTE

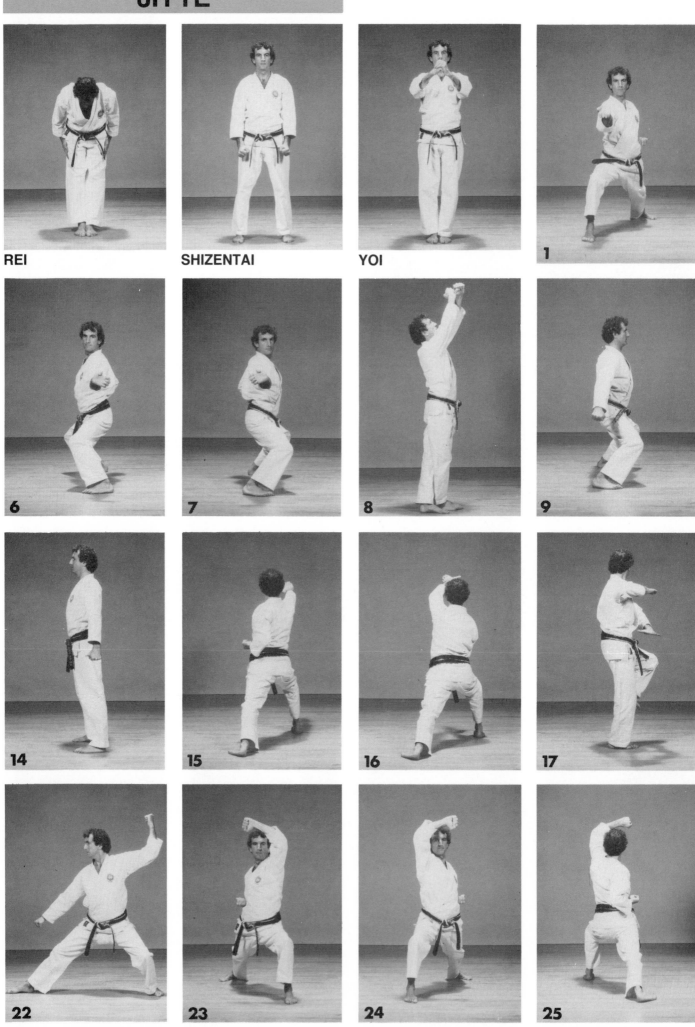

REI SHIZENTAI YOI 1

6 7 8 9

14 15 16 17

22 23 24 25

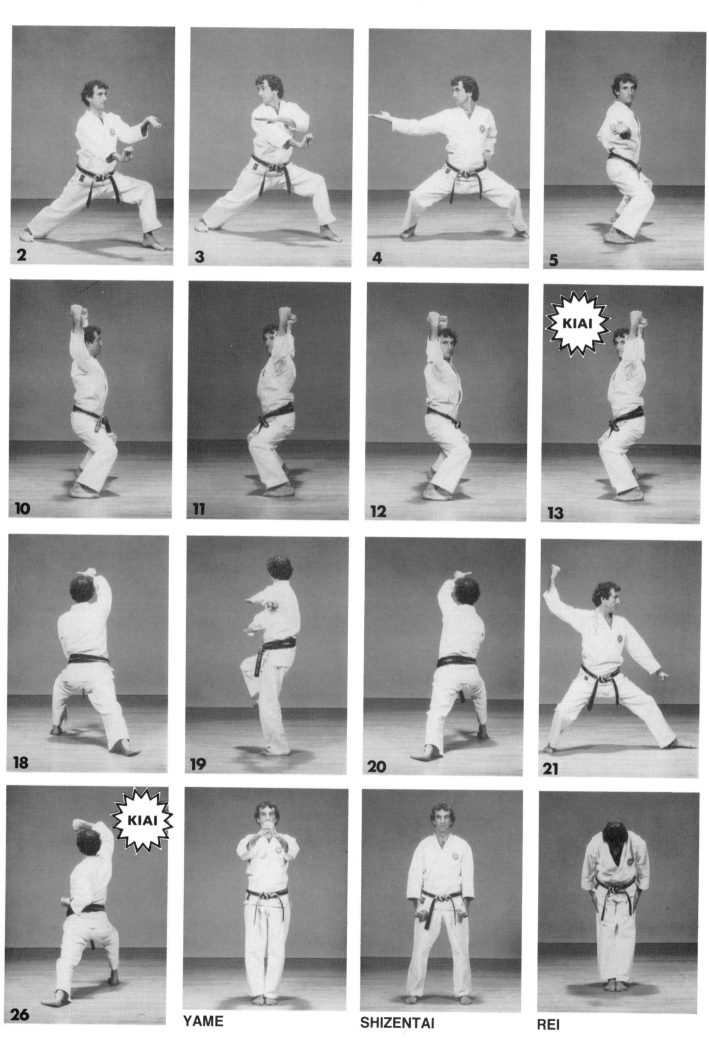

2

3

4

5

10

11

12

13 **KIAI**

18

19

20

21

26 **KIAI**

YAME

SHIZENTAI

REI

"MIGI JŌDAN AGE UKE"

APPLICATION FOR MOVEMENT 1

BLOCKING A LUNGE PUNCH WITH A RIGHT
PALM HEEL BLOCK

BLOCKING A REVERSE PUNCH
WITH A LEFT PALM HEEL BLOCK

CATCHING THE ATTACKING UPPER PUNCH

DEFLECTING AND BLOCKING WITH
MIGI TEKUBI KAKE UKE

COUNTER ATTACKING WITH A
RISING PALM HEEL STRIKE

APPLICATIONS FOR MOVEMENTS 15–20

1 BLOCKING—SHUTŌ

2 GRABBING BO

3 TWISTING BO

4 BREAKING GRIP

5 PULLING BACK

6 ATTACKING WITH BO

7 TWISTING

8 TAKING BO AWAY FROM ATTACKER

APPLICATION FOR MOVEMENT 23

BLOCKING A LUNGE PUNCH

MOVING IN AND GRABBING

BREAKING THE BALANCE

TWISTING

THROWING

"MIGI HAITŌ UCHI"

TEKKI SHODAN

鉄騎初段

INTRODUCTION

Tekki Shodan is basically a "training" Kata and makes generous use of "Kiba Dachi", which should be strong and stable at all times. The hips should remain well set when performing the "Returning Wave" kick known as "Nami Ashi" or "Nami Gaeshi". Previously known as "Naihanchi" this Kata was renamed "Tekki" by Funakoshi, and has three forms — Shodan, Nidan and Sandan. This Kata is more difficult than it looks and requires mastery of tension and relaxation.

The system for explaining the Kata is as follows:

On page 122 you will find a schematic diagram of Tekki Shodan and a picture of the camera used to photograph all the main movements which appear at the top of the following pages. The camera position remains constant and the practitioner begins and ends his Kata facing the camera. If in retreat when his movements are obscured by his back view, we have photographed him from the side or front and this has been clearly marked.

For many years now, throughout Shotokan Karate, students have been taught to move forward, back, left or right, or to "45°". This applies to basics, Kata and all six forms of basic Kumite.

In this book, to assist in the explanation of Kata, as far as DIRECTION is concerned, I have likened these moves to the points of the compass.

At the top left hand side of page 122 will be found a photograph of a compass showing the four cardinal points of North, South, East and West, together with the four lesser ones of South East, South West, etc., eight in all — the same eight that cover almost every Shotokan move taught today.

On the top right hand side of the page is a simplified version showing the eight directions. With the practitioner standing in the centre, facing the camera, forward is "One", back is "Two", his left is "Three", and his right "Four".

Once this simple eight point system has been understood, the most advanced Kata can be easily understood — directionally speaking.

To summarize then — the photograph at the top of the page is the completed move.

The photographs in the centre of the page show the completed moves, possibly at different angles, to aid understanding, plus the midway points. Finally, the practical application is shown at the bottom of the page and a complete summary of Tekki Shodan appears on page 140.

There is no substitute for a good teacher and this book is merely intended to compliment that teaching — not replace it.

The following ten elements of Kata, as taught by Kanazawa Sensei, should be borne in mind at all times. Without them, the Kata will be meaningless.

YOI NO KISIN — the spirit of getting ready. The concentration of will and mind against the opponent as a preliminary to the movements of the Kata.

INYO — the active and passive. Always keeping in mind both attack and defence.

CHIKARA NO KYOJAKU — the manner of using strength. The degree of power used for each movement and position in Kata.

WAZA NO KANKYU — the speed of movement. The speed used for each movement and position in Kata.

TAI NO SHINSHUKU — the degree of expansion or contraction. The degree of expansion or contraction of the body in each movement and position in Kata.

KOKYU — breathing. Breath control related to the posture and movement in Kata*.

TYAKUGAN — the aiming points. In Kata you must keep the purpose of the movement in mind.

KIAI — shouting. Shouting at set points in Kata to demonstrate the martial spirit.

KEITAI NO HOJI — correct positioning. Correct positioning in movement and stance.

ZANSHIN — remaining on guard. Remaining on guard at the completion of the Kata (i.e. back to 'Yoi') until told to relax 'Enoy'.

*N.B. KOKYU — Breathing in Kata plays a very important part towards its correct execution. Inhalation takes place via the nose and exhalation through the mouth. In the following Kata, where a "sequence" of techniques occurs, inhalation is immediately followed by exhalation spread over the number of techniques involved, which often are performed in rapid succession.

鉄騎初段

"HIDARI JŌDAN URA ZUKI"

SCHEMATIC DIAGRAM OF TEKKI SHODAN AND DIRECTIONAL ANALYSIS

MOVE	DIRECTION
1	4
2	4
3	4
4	3
5	3
6	3
7	3
8	1
9	1
10	3
11	4
12	3
13	3
14	3
15	3
16	4
17	4
18	4
19	4
20	1
21	1
22	4
23	3
24	4
25	4

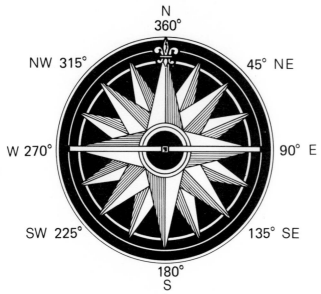

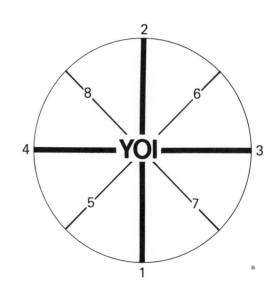

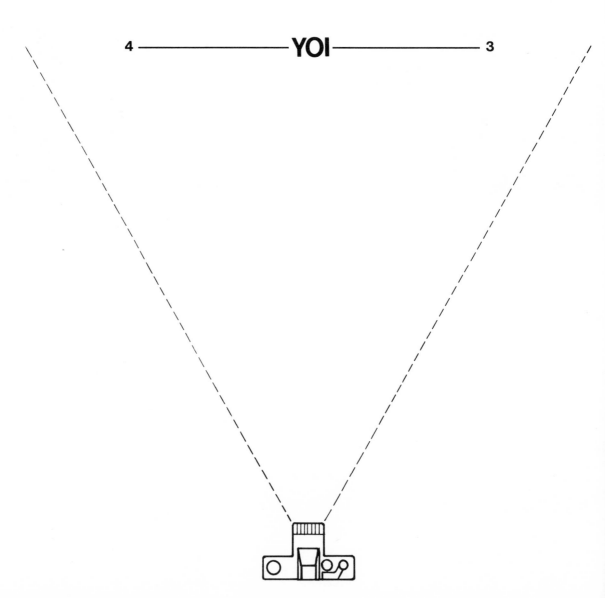

SHIZENTAI

YOI

REI

SHIZENTAI

MIDWAY

YOI

After bowing in Heisoku Dachi move the right foot to the right into Shizentai. From this position, move the right foot back to the left one simultaneously opening both hands and bringing them to the centre of the body at stomach height. The left hand should be in front of the right and the legs straight.

KŌSA DACHI

HAISHU UKE

YOI

KŌSA DACHI

MIDWAY
FUMIKOMI

HAISHU UKE

MOVEMENT 1
Kōsa Dachi

SHIFT 1: At the same time perform the following actions. Turn the head to direction 4, bend the right knee, drop the body and step over the right leg with the left placing the ball of the left foot on the floor in line with the right.

SPEED: Fast with half power.

BREATHING: Commence breathing in through nose.

DIRECTION:

MOVEMENT 2:
Haishu Uke

STANCE: Kiba Dachi.

SHIFT: Keeping the head facing direction 4, swing the right leg up in front of the body after first crossing the arms. As the leg comes down into straddle stance attacking Fumikomi, the right arm blocks with a backhand block to the attaching punch.

SPEED: Fast with focus.

BREATHING: In through nose and half out.

DIRECTION:

BLOCKING A LUNGE PUNCH

COUNTER ATTACKING WITH A HOOK PUNCH

SOKUMEN ENPI

KŌSHI GAMAE

MIDWAY

SOKUMEN ENPI

MIDWAY

KŌSHI GAMAE

MOVEMENT 3
Sokumen Enpi

STANCE: Kiba Dachi.

SHIFT 3: Swing the left elbow laterally to the right, at the same time, withdraw the right hand, bending at the elbow, striking the right palm with the left elbow.

SPEED: Fast with focus.

BREATHING: Out through mouth.

DIRECTION:

MOVEMENT 4
Kōshi Gamae

STANCE: Kiba Dachi.

SHIFT 4: Move the right arm to the side of the body, making a fist, with the palm up. Allow the left fist to position itself vertically over the top of the right. In doing this, turn the head 180° to the left.

SPEED: Fast with half power.

BREATHING: In fast through nose.

DIRECTION:

BLOCKING A LUNGE PUNCH

COUNTER ATTACKING WITH A ROUNDHOUSE ELBOW STRIKE

HIDARI GEDAN BARAI

MIGI KAGE ZUKI

KŌSHI GAMAE

MIDWAY

HIDARI GEDAN BARAI

MIDWAY

MOVEMENT 5
Hidari Gedan Barai

STANCE: Kiba Dachi.

SHIFT 5: Move the left arm across the body and perform a left downward block.

SPEED: Fast with focus.

BREATHING: Half out through mouth.

DIRECTION: 3

MOVEMENT 6
Migi Kage Zuki

STANCE: Kiba Dachi.

SHIFT 6: Pull the left fist smartly to the waist executing a hook punch with the right arm.

SPEED: Fast with focus.

BREATHING: Remaining half out through mouth.

DIRECTION: 3

BLOCKING A FRONT KICK ATTACK

SLIDING IN AND COUNTER ATTACKING WITH A HOOK PUNCH

KŌSA DACHI

MIGI UCHI UKE

**MIGI
KAGE ZUKI**

KŌSA DACHI

FUMIKOMI

MIGI UCHI UKE

MOVEMENT 7
Kōsa Dachi

STANCE: —

SHIFT 7: Step with the right foot into Kōsa Dachi keeping the arms in the same position as in movement 6.

SPEED: Slowly — no power.

BREATHING: Slowly — long inhalation.

DIRECTION: 3

MOVEMENT 8
Migi Uchi Uke

STANCE: Kiba Dachi.

SHIFT 8: Transfer the body weight onto the right foot, swing the left leg up in front and down into Kiba Dachi performing Fumikomi. At the same time swing the right arm to the left ear and then forward to execute an inside forearm block.

SPEED: Fast with focus.

BREATHING: Out through mouth.

DIRECTION: 1

**BLOCKING A MIDDLE LUNGE
PUNCH WITH AN INSIDE
FOREARM BLOCK**

**BLOCKING AN UPPER REVERSE
PUNCH AND SIMULTANEOUSLY
PUNCHING TO THE MID SECTION**

**STRIKING WITH A MIDDLE
ROUNDHOUSE
ELBOW STRIKE**

HIDARI JŌDAN URA ZUKI

SOKUMEN UKE

9A — ARMS CROSSED

9B — JŌDAN NAGASHI UKE

9 — HIDARI JŌDAN URA ZUKI

MIDWAY HIDARI NAMI ASHI

MOVEMENT 9
Hidari Jōdan Ura Zuki

STANCE: Kiba Dachi

SHIFT 9: From Migi Uchi Uke, cross the arms in front of the body and perform Jōdan Nagashi Uke (blocking with the left — punching with the right) then thrust the left fist forward in a close punch bringing the right backfist to the left elbow.

SPEED: Fast with focus.

BREATHING: In through nose, out through mouth.

DIRECTION: 1

MOVEMENT 10
Sokumen Uke

STANCE: Kiba Dachi.

SHIFT 10: Turn the head 90° to the left, perform a left Nami Ashi (returning wave kick) and complete the augmented inside block known as Sokumen Uke.

SPEED: Fast with focus.

BREATHING: In through nose, out through mouth.

DIRECTION: 3

BLOCKING A LUNGE PUNCH

COUNTER ATTACKING WITH A PUNCH TO THE MID SECTION

COMPLETING THE COUNTER ATTACK WITH A CLOSE PUNCH TO THE FACE

SOKUMEN UKE

KŌSHI GAMAE

SOKUMEN UKE

MIDWAY
MIGI NAMI ASHI

SOKUMEN UKE

KŌSHI GAMAE

**MOVEMENT 11
Sokumen Uke**

STANCE: Kiba Dachi.

SHIFT 11: Block with the same arm as movement 10 but to the right by — turning the head to the right, performing a right Nami Ashi and blocking the Sokumen Uke.

SPEED: Fast with focus.

BREATHING: In through the nose, out through the mouth.

DIRECTION:

**MOVEMENT 12
Kōshi Gamae**

STANCE 12: Bring the right fist to the waist palm up, with the left fist vertically over it. At the same time, turn the head sharply to the left.

SPEED: Fast — half power.

BREATHING: In through nose.

DIRECTION:

**EVADING A THRUST KICK
ATTACK TO THE KNEE JOINT**

BLOCKING A REVERSE PUNCH

MOROTE ZUKI

HAISHU UKE

KŌSHI GAMAE

MIDWAY

MOROTE ZUKI

MIDWAY

MOVEMENT 13
Morote Zuki

STANCE: Kiba Dachi.

SHIFT 13: Thrust the left fist to the left and perform a middle punch, augmenting it with the right arm which should be a little lower than the left when the technique is completed.

SPEED: Fast with focus.

BREATHING: Out through mouth with Kiai.

DIRECTION:

MOVEMENT 14
Haishu Uke

STANCE: Kiba Dachi.

SHIFT 14: Move the left arm under the right one, open the left hand and perform a left backhand block as illustrated.

SPEED: Slowly — no power.

BREATHING: Long inhalation through nose.

DIRECTION:

SLIDING INSIDE THE OPPONENT'S GUARD AND EXECUTING AN AUGMENTED MID SECTION PUNCH

SOKUMEN ENPI

KŌSHI GAMAE

14

HAISHU UKE

MIDWAY

15

SOKUMEN ENPI

16

KŌSHI GAMAE

MOVEMENT 15
Sokumen Enpi

STANCE: Kiba Dachi.

SHIFT 15: Strike the left palm with the right elbow, moving both towards each other.

SPEED: Fast with focus.

BREATHING: Out through mouth.

DIRECTION: 3

MOVEMENT 16:
Kōshi Gamae

STANCE: Kiba Dachi.

SHIFT 16: Turn the head smartly 180° to the right, bring the left fist to the waist (palm up) and the right one vertically over it.

SPEED: Fast — half power.

BREATHING: In through nose.

DIRECTION: 4

BLOCKING A LUNGE PUNCH WITH A BACKHAND BLOCK

COUNTER ATTACKING WITH A HOOK PUNCH

Tekki Shodan　**131**

MIGI GEDAN BARAI

HIDARI KAGE ZUKI

KŌSHI GAMAE

MIGI GEDAN BARAI

MIDWAY

HIDARI KAGE ZUKI

MOVEMENT 17
Migi Gedan Barai

STANCE: Kiba Dachi.

SHIFT 17: Execute a right downward block.

SPEED: Fast with focus.

BREATHING: Half out through mouth.

DIRECTION: 4

MOVEMENT 18
Hidari Kage Zuki

STANCE: Kiba Dachi.

SHIFT 18: Perform a left hook punch pulling the right fist sharply to the waist.

SPEED: Fast with Kime.

BREATHING: Remaining half out through mouth.

DIRECTION: 4

USING A DOWNWARD BLOCK TO PARRY A FRONT KICK

RETALIATING WITH A HOOK PUNCH TO THE SOLAR PLEXUS

KŌSA DACHI

HIDARI UCHI UKE

19

KŌSA DACHI

20A

20B

FUMIKOMI

20

HIDARI UCHI UKE

MOVEMENT 19
Kōsa Dachi

STANCE: —

SHIFT 19: Maintain the hook punch position and step across to the right with the left leg, taking the left foot just over the right one.

SPEED: Slowly — no power.

BREATHING: Long inhalation through nose.

DIRECTION: 4

MOVEMENT 20
Hidari Uchi Uke

STANCE: Kiba Dachi.

SHIFT 20: Take the body weight on the left foot, look to the front and swing the right leg up and down into straddle stance performing a stamping kick. Execute a left inside forearm block at the same time.

SPEED: Fast with focus.

BREATHING: Out through mouth.

DIRECTION: 1

DEFENDING AGAINST A LUNGE PUNCH WITH "UCHI UKE"

ATTACKER WITHDRAWS RIGHT HAND AND PREPARES TO ATTACK AGAIN

"U" PUNCH ATTACK BEING BLOCKED WITH AGE UKE AND GEDAN BARAI

MIGI JŌDAN URA ZUKI

MIGI SOKUMEN UKE

CROSSED ARMS

**MIGI JŌDAN
NAGASHI UKE**

**MIGI JŌDAN URA
ZUKI**

MIGI NAMI ASHI

**MOVEMENT 21
Migi Jōdan Ura Zuki**

STANCE: Kiba Dachi.

SHIFT 21: Cross the arms in front of the body and perform Nagashi Uke. Follow this with a right upper close punch

SPEED: Fast with focus.

BREATHING: In through nose, out through mouth.

DIRECTION:

**MOVEMENT 22
Migi Sokumen Uke**

STANCE: Kiba Dachi.

SHIFT 22: Turn the head 90° to the right, dispatch a right Nami Ashi followed by a right Sokumen Uke.

SPEED: Fast with focus.

**RIGHT FIST INVERTED
DELIVERING AN AUGMENTED
"CLOSE" PUNCH**

**MIGI SOKUMEN
UKE**

BREATHING: In through nose, out through mouth.

DIRECTION:

MIGI SOKUMEN UKE

KŌSHI GAMAE

HIDARI NAMI ASHI

HIDARI NAMI ASHI

MIGI SOKUMEN UKE

KŌSHI GAMAE

MOVEMENT 23
Migi Sokumen Uke

STANCE: Kiba Dachi.

SHIFT 23: Turn the head 180° to the left executing a left Nami Ashi (returning wave kick) and perform another Migi Sokumen Uke.

SPEED: Fast with focus.

BREATHING: In through nose, out through mouth.

DIRECTION: ⸻3

MOVEMENT 24
Kōshi Gamae

STANCE: Kiba Dachi

SHIFT 24: Again, turn the head 180° to the right (Direction 4) bringing the left fist to the waist and the right one vertically over it.

SPEED: Fast, half power.

BREATHING: In through nose.

DIRECTION: 4⸻

BLOCKING A LUNGE PUNCH

MOROTE ZUKI

YAME

KŌSHI GAMAE

MIDWAY

MOROTE ZUKI

MIDWAY

**MOVEMENT 25
Morote Zuki**

STANCE: Kiba Dachi.

SHIFT 25: Thrust the right fist to the right followed simultaneously by the left in an augmenting capacity. The left is slightly lower than the right.

SPEED: Fast with focus and Kiai.

BREATHING: Out through mouth.

DIRECTION: 4

SHIFT: To move into Yame, withdraw the right leg to the left simultaneously opening the hands (palms down) and moving them back into the centre of the body. The head turns to the front in time with the hands and both reach the end of their travel, as the feet touch each other.

AUGMENTED PUNCH TO THE MID SECTION

SHIZENTAI

REI

YAME

SHIZENTAI

REI

MOVEMENT
The Shizentai position is regained by moving the right foot to the right and crossing the arms in front of the body.

MOVEMENT
In order to bow in Heisoku Dachi, bring the right foot to the left — the hands to the sides, and "Rei".

AN ADVANCED VARIATION OF THE AUGMENTED PUNCH USING THE FORWARD ARM TO PARRY THE ATTACK AND THE REAR ARM TO DELIVER THE BLOW. USUALLY PERFORMED WHILST SLIDING IN.

"HIDARI NAMI ASHI"

"MOROTE ZUKI"

TEKKI SHODAN

REI

SHIZENTAI

YOI

1

6

7

8

9

14

15

16

17

22

23

24

25

2

3

4

5

10

11

12

13

18

19

20

21

YAME

SHIZENTAI

REI

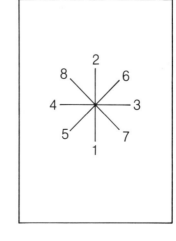

TEKKI NIDAN

鉄騎弐段

INTRODUCTION

Tekki Nidan like Shodan and Sandan is basically a "Training" Kata and makes generous use of "Kiba Dachi" which should be strong and stable at all times. It was created by Master Itosu from Shuri-Te being modelled on Tekki Shodan. Thought by some to have originated in China, the horizontal line in which the techniques are performed suggests fighting in a boat, or an alleyway — perhaps even with one's back against the wall. The name Naihanchi was changed by Funakoshi for Tekki and has endured ever since.

The system for explaining the Kata is as follows:

On page 146 you will find a schematic diagram of Tekki Nidan and a picture of the camera used to photograph all the main movements which appear at the top of the following pages. The camera position remains constant and the practitioner begins and ends his Kata facing the camera. If in retreat when his movements are obscured by his back view, we have photographed him from the side or front and this has been clearly marked.

For many years now, throughout Shotokan Karate, students have been taught to move forward, back, to left or right, or to "45°". This applies to basics, Kata and all six forms of basic Kumite.

In this book, to assist in the explanation of Kata, as far as DIRECTION is concerned, I have likened these moves to the points of the compass.

At the top left hand side of page 146 will be found a photograph of a compass showing the four cardinal points of North, South, East and West, together with the four lesser ones of South East, South West, etc., eight in all — the same eight that cover almost every Shotokan move taught today.

On the top right hand side of the page is a simplified version showing the eight directions. With the practitioner standing in the centre, facing the camera, forward is "One", back is "Two", his left is "Three", and his right "Four".

Once this simple eight point system has been grasped, the most advanced Kata can be easily understood — directionally speaking.

To summarize then — the photograph at the top of the page is the completed move.

The photographs in the centre of the page show the completed moves, possibly at different angles, to aid understanding, plus the midway points. Finally, the practical application is shown at the bottom of the page and a complete summary of Tekki Nidan appears on page 164.

There is no substitute for a good teacher and this book is merely intended to compliment that teaching — not replace it.

The following ten elements of Kata, as taught by Kanazawa Sensei, should be borne in mind at all times. Without them, the Kata will be meaningless.

YOI NO KISIN — the spirit of getting ready. The concentration of will and mind against the opponent as a preliminary to the movements of the Kata.

INYO — the active and passive. Always keeping in mind both attack and defence.

CHIKARA NO KYOJAKU — the manner of using strength. The degree of power used for each movement and position in Kata.

WAZA NO KANKYU — the speed of movement. The speed used for each movement and position in Kata.

TAI NO SHINSHUKU — the degree of expansion or contraction. The degree of expansion or contraction of the body in each movement and position in Kata.

KOKYU — breathing. Breath control related to the posture and movement in Kata*.

TYAKUGAN — the aiming points. In Kata you must keep the purpose of the movement in mind.

KIAI — shouting. Shouting at set points in Kata to demonstrate the martial spirit.

KEITAI NO HOJI — correct positioning. Correct positioning in movement and stance.

ZANSHIN — remaining on guard. Remaining on guard at the completion of the Kata (i.e. back to 'Yoi') until told to relax 'Enoy'.

*N.B. KOKYU — Breathing in Kata plays a very important part towards its correct execution. Inhalation takes place via the nose and exhalation through the mouth. In the following Kata, where a "sequence" of techniques occurs, inhalation is immediately followed by exhalation spread over the number of techniques involved, which often are performed in rapid succession.

鉄騎弐段

"MIGI JŌDAN URA ZUKI"

SCHEMATIC DIAGRAM
AND DIRECTIONAL ANALYSIS
OF TEKKI NIDAN

MOVE	DIRECTION
1	4
2	4
3	1
4	4
5	3
6	3
7	1
8	3
9	5
10	5
11	1
12	4
13	4
14	4
15	1
16	1
17	7
18	7
19	1
20	3
21	3
22	3
23	1
24	1

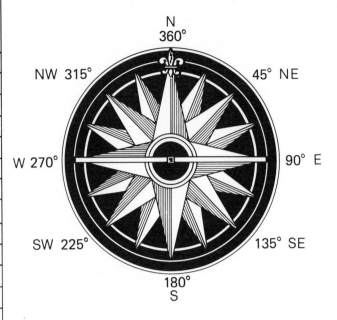

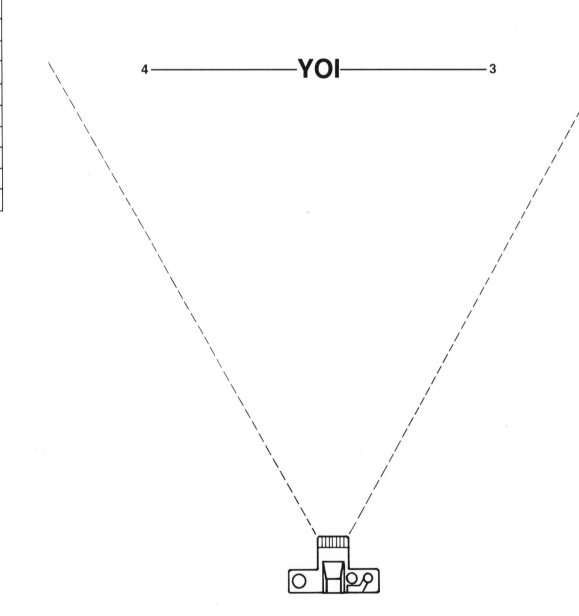

REI

YOI

REI

MIDWAY

YOI

After bowing in Heisoku Dachi, move
the right foot to the right into Shizentai.
Once in the "Yoi", or ready position,
the practitioner remains "On Guard"
and alert, ready for the attack that will
eventually come.

MOVEMENT 1	**MOVEMENT 2**

RYO HIJI HARAI AGE

SOKUMEN UKE DŌJI FUMIKOMI

YOI

MIDWAY

RYO HIJI HARAI AGE

MIDWAY

MOVEMENT 1
Ryo Hiji Harai Age

STANCE: Kōsa Dachi.

SHIFT 1: Taking the body weight on the right leg, step to the right with the left foot, stepping over the right foot and placing the ball of the left foot on the floor as indicated. At the same time, both fists should rise to the chest leaving the arms horizontal and the head facing Direction 4.

SPEED: Slowly — half power.

BREATHING: Long inhalation.

DIRECTION: 4

MOVEMENT 2
Sokumen Uke — Dōji Fumikomi

STANCE: Kiba Dachi.

SHIFT 2: Thrust both arms up in front of the face, simultaneously swinging the right leg up to the front. Bring the right foot down into straddle stance performing a stamping kick, whilst blocking with Sokumen Uke.

SPEED: Fast with focus.

BREATHING: Out through mouth.

DIRECTION: 4

ATTACKER APPROACHES FROM BEHIND

BEAR HUG

DROPPING DOWN AND BREAKING THE GRIP

COUNTERING WITH AN AUGMENTED REVERSE ELBOW STRIKE

GEDAN SOTO UDE UKE

SOKUMEN SOETE GEDAN UCHI UDE UKE

SOKUMEN UKE DŌJI FUMIKOMI   MIDWAY

GEDAN SOTO UDE UKE   MIDWAY

MOVEMENT 3
Gedan Soto Ude Uke

STANCE: Kōsa Dachi.

SHIFT 3: Step across and over the right foot with the left one, bringing the right arm down into a lower outside forearm block. The left hand should act in an augmenting capacity being placed in the crook of the right arm.

SPEED: Fast with focus.

BREATHING: Out through mouth.

DIRECTION:

MOVEMENT 4
Sokumen Soete Gedan Uchi Ude Uke

STANCE: Kiba Dachi.

SHIFT 4: Step to the right with the right foot into straddle stance and keeping the arms in the same position as in movement 3, swing them both to the right performing an augmented lower inside forearm block. N.B. The right hand stays palm up and does not twist over and back. (Through 180°.)

SPEED: Fast with focus.

BREATHING:
Out through mouth.

DIRECTION:

BLOCKING A LUNGE PUNCH

BLOCKING A MAE GERI FRONTAL ATTACK

BLOCKING A MAE GERI SIDE ATTACK

RYO HIJI HARAI AGE

SOKUMEN UKE DŌJI FUMIKOMI

SOKUMEN SOETE GEDAN UCHI UDE UKE

MIDWAY

RYO HIJI HARAI AGE

MIDWAY

MOVEMENT 5
Ryo Hiji Harai Age

STANCE: Heisoku Dachi.

SHIFT 5: Move the left foot to the right in Heisoku Dachi whilst raising the arms in front of the body to chest height. The backs of the fists remain upwards and the head turns slowly to the left.

SPEED: Slowly half power.

BREATHING: Long inhalation through nose.

DIRECTION: 3

MOVEMENT 6
Sokumen Uke Dōji Fumikomi

STANCE: Kiba Dachi.

SHIFT 6: Swing the arms up in front of the face together with the left leg bringing it down into straddle stance, performing a stamping kick and augmented Chudan block.

SPEED: Fast with focus.

BREATHING: Out through mouth.

DIRECTION: 3

BLOCKING A LUNGE PUNCH

COUNTER ATTACKING WITH KIZAMI ZUKI

GEDAN SOTO UDE UKE

SOKUMEN SOETE GEDAN UCHI UDE UKE

6

MIDWAY

7

MIDWAY

**SOKUMEN UKE
DŌJI FUMIKOMI**

GEDAN SOTO UDE UKE

SHIFT 8: Stepping to the left, with the left foot into straddle stance, swing both arms and perform an augmented lower inside forearm block. Keep the palm of the left fist facing upwards.

SPEED: Fast with focus.

BREATHING: Out through mouth.

**MOVEMENT 7
Gedan Soto Ude Uke**

STANCE: Kōsa Dachi.

SHIFT 7: With the right foot, step across and over the left into Kōsa Dachi executing a lower outside forearm block. The head faces Direction 1.

SPEED: Fast with focus.

BREATHING: Out through mouth.

DIRECTION:

1

**MOVEMENT 8
Sokumen Soete Gedan Uchi Ude Uke**

STANCE: Kiba Dachi.

DIRECTION:

3

BLOCKING A FRONTAL SIDE THRUST KICK

1

BLOCKING A SIDE THRUST KICK FROM THE SIDE

2

DRIVING IN AND ATTACKING WITH A KIZAMI ZUKI TO THE FACE

SOETE KŌSHI GAMAE

SOETE SOKUMEN UKE

8

SOKUMEN SOETE GEDAN UCHI UDE UKE

MIDWAY

9

SOETE KŌSHI GAMAE

MIDWAY

MOVEMENT 9
Soete Kōshi Gamae

STANCE: Kiba Dachi.

SHIFT 9: Movement 9 is a preparatory position for the block to follow and consists of placing the right vertical fist in the palm of the left hand as illustrated.

SPEED: Fast with half power.

BREATHING: Fast inhalation through nose.

DIRECTION: head facing 45°.

MOVEMENT 10
Soete Sokumen Uke

STANCE: Kiba Dachi.

SHIFT 10: This technique is a variation of an augmented inside forearm block performed here by swinging both arms to a 45° position. The tip of the middle finger should be level with the bottom of the fist.

SPEED: Fast with focus.

BREATHING: Out through mouth.

DIRECTION: Blocking at attack at 45°.

PREPARING TO ATTACK

ATTACKING WITH A LUNGE PUNCH

BLOCKING A LUNGE PUNCH

SOETE MAE ENPI DŌJI FUMIKOMI

SOKUMEN TATE SHUTŌ UKE

SOETE SOKUMEN UKE   MIDWAY

SOETE MAE ENPI DŌJI FUMIKOMI   MIDWAY

MOVEMENT 11
Soete Mae Enpi — Dōji Fumikomi

STANCE: Kiba Dachi.

SHIFT 11: As the right leg swings up to the front ready for Dōji Fumikomi, pull the right arm back to the waist keeping the left open hand to it. Then, bringing the right leg into Kiba Dachi, deliver a front elbow strike augmenting it with the left hand.

SPEED: Fast with focus.

BREATHING: In through nose, out through mouth.

DIRECTION:

1

MOVEMENT 12
Sokumen Tate Shutō Uke

STANCE: Kiba Dachi.

SHIFT 12: Swing the right arm in a wide arc to block with a vertical knife hand block to the right (Direction 4) as the left fist is pulled back to the waist in the inverted position.

SPEED: Slowly — focus with half power.

BREATHING: Long inhalation.

DIRECTION: 4

GRABBING THE ARM AND BREAKING THE BALANCE

DEALING SIMULTANEOUSLY WITH AN ATTACKER FROM THE REAR

EXECUTING A STAMPING KICK TO THE KNEE JOINT

FINISHING WITH AN UPPER ELBOW STRIKE

HIDARI KAGE ZUKI

YOKO SASHI ASHI

SŌKUMEN TATE SHUTŌ UKE

MIDWAY

HIDARI KAGE ZUKI

MIDWAY

MOVEMENT 13
Hidari Kage Zuki

STANCE: Kiba Dachi.

SHIFT 13: Perform a left hook punch as the right fist is snapped smartly back to the waist. The punching fist never protrudes beyond the body line — distance is gained by sliding in towards the opponent.

SPEED: Fast with focus.

BREATHING: Out through mouth.

DIRECTION:

MOVEMENT 14
Yoko Sashi Ashi

STANCE: Kōsa Dachi.

SHIFT 14: Step to the right with the left foot and across the right one as indicated. The arms do not change their position.

SPEED: Slowly — no power.

BREATHING: Long inhalation.

DIRECTION:

BLOCKING A LUNGE PUNCH

SLIDING IN AND ATTACKING THE STERNUM WITH AN ELBOW STRIKE

BLOCKING WITH AN INSIDE FOREARM BLOCK

MOVEMENT 15   MOVEMENT 16

HIDARI UCHI UKE DŌJI FUMIKOMI

MIGI JŌDAN URA ZUKI

14

YOKO SASHI ASHI

MIDWAY

15

HIDARI UCHI UKE DŌJI FUMIKOMI

MIDWAY (A)

MIDWAY (B)
MIGI JŌDAN NAGASHI UKE

MOVEMENT 15
Hidari Uchi Uke — Dōji Fumikomi

STANCE: Kiba Dachi.

SHIFT 15: Now perform a stamping kick with the right leg and an inside forearm block with the left arm. In executing this technique, one should endeavour to twist the upper and lower body in opposite directions i.e. the upper body to the right and the lower to the left.

SPEED: Fast with focus.

BREATHING: Out through mouth.

DIRECTION:

MOVEMENT 16
Migi Jōdan Ura Zuki

STANCE: Kiba Dachi.

SHIFT 16: Crossing the right arm in front of the left, block an upper punching attack by performing an upper sweeping block with the right arm and a middle punching attack with the left arm, now, thrust the right inverted fist in a straight line to attack with an augmented close punch.

SPEED: Fast with focus and Kiai.

BREATHING: Out through mouth.

DIRECTION:

2

PUNCHING TO THE MID SECTION

3

FINISHING WITH A CLOSE PUNCH TO THE CHIN

SOETE KŌSHI GAMAE

SOETE SOKUMEN UKE

MIGI JŌDAN URA ZUKI   MIDWAY   **SOETE KŌSHI GAMAE**   MIDWAY

**MOVEMENT 17
Soete Kōshi Gamae**

STANCE: Kiba Dachi.

SHIFT 17: Turn the head 45° and bring the hands to the right hand side of the body as illustrated.

SPEED: Fast-half power.

BREATHING: In through nose.

DIRECTION:
Head facing 45°.

**MOVEMENT 18
Soete Sokumen Uke**

STANCE: Kiba Dachi.

SHIFT 18: Swing both arms to the left and perform an augmented inside forearm block at 45°.

SPEED: Fast with focus.

BREATHING: Out through mouth.

DIRECTION:

**STRIKING A SECOND ATTACKER
APPROACHING FROM BEHIND WITH AN
AUGMENTED REVERSE ELBOW STRIKE**

SOETE MAE ENPI DŌJI FUMIKOMI

SOKUMEN TATE SHUTŌ UKE

SOETE SOKUMEN UKE

MIDWAY

SOETE MAE ENPI DŌJI FUMIKOMI

MIDWAY

MOVEMENT 19
Soete Mae Enpi Dōji Fumikomi

STANCE: Kiba Dachi.

SHIFT 19: Repeat Movement 11, but on the opposite side.

SPEED: Fast with focus.

BREATHING: In through nose — out through mouth.

DIRECTION:

1

MOVEMENT 20
Sokumen Tate Shutō Uke

STANCE: Kiba Dachi.

SHIFT 20: Swing the left arm in a wide arc to perform a vertical knife hand block.

SPEED: Slowly — focus with half power.

BREATHING: Long inhalation through nose.

DIRECTION:

3

BLOCKING A LUNGE PUNCH

COUNTER ATTACKING WITH A REVERSE PUNCH

MIGI KAGE ZUKI

YOKO SASHI ASHI

20

SOKUMEN TATE SHUTŌ UKE

MIDWAY

21

MIGI KAGE ZUKI

MIDWAY

MOVEMENT 21
Migi Kage Zuki

STANCE: Kiba Dachi.

SHIFT 21: Punch in a circular motion with the right arm executing a hook punch to the mid section.

SPEED: Fast with focus.

BREATHING: Out through mouth.

DIRECTION: 3

MOVEMENT 22
Yoko Sashi Ashi

STANCE: Kōsa Dachi.

SHIFT 22: Step across the left foot with the right maintaining the arm position from Movement 21.

SPEED: Slowly — no power.

BREATHING: Long inhalation through nose.

DIRECTION: (direction diagram) 3

1

BLOCKING A LUNGE PUNCH

2

ATTACKER PULLS BACK PUNCHING ARM .

MIGI UCHI UKE DŌJI FUMIKOMI

HIDARI JŌDAN URA ZUKI

KIAI

22
YOKO SASHI ASHI

MIDWAY

23
MIGI UCHI UKE DŌJI FUMIKOMI

MIDWAY (A)

MIDWAY (B)
HIDARI JŌDAN NAGASHI UKE

MOVEMENT 23
Migi Uchi Uke — Dōji Fumikomi

STANCE: Kiba Dachi.

SHIFT 23: Repeat Movement 15, but on the opposite side.

SPEED: Fast with focus.

BREATHING: Out through mouth.

DIRECTION:

1

MOVEMENT 24
Hidari Jōdan Ura Zuki

STANCE: Kiba Dachi.

SHIFT 24: Repeat Movement 16 but on the opposite side.

SPEED: Fast with focus and Kiai.

BREATHING: In through nose — out through mouth.

DIRECTION:

1

3
AND ATTACKS AGAIN WITH A "U" PUNCH

4
STRIKING THE CHIN WITH AN UPPER CLOSE PUNCH

YAME

REI

KIAI

HIDARI JŌDAN URA ZUKI

MIDWAY

YAME

REI

The Shizentai position is regained by moving the right foot to the left and crossing the arms in front of the body as illustrated.

In order to bow in Heisoku Dachi, move the right foot to the left one, bring the open hands to the sides of the body and "Rei".

Kata begins and ends with courtesy, as indeed does all aspects of Karate-Dō.

AUTHOR'S NOTE:

In Karate training, many things that appear simple at first, often turn out to be the most difficult to master, none more so, than the customary "Bow".

To Orientals, the Bow is not just a bending of the body in a forward direction, as it is with many Westerners.

It is a deliberate action — a method of communication, embodying the deepest of spiritual connotations.

It is a salutation, that goes far beyond the act of shaking hands. Only after years of practice, can the "Rei" take on the correct shape and form and so convey what is meant.

"RYO HIJI HARAI AGE"

"DŌJI FUMIKOMI"

"SOETE SOKUMEN UKE"

TEKKI NIDAN

REI   YOI   1   2

7   8   9   10

15   16 KIAI   17   18

23   24 KIAI   YAME   REI

TEKKI SANDAN

鉄騎三段

INTRODUCTION

Tekki Sandan like Shodan and Nidan is basically a "Training" Kata and makes generous use of "Kiba Dachi" which should be strong and stable at all times. It was created by Master Itosu from Shuri-Te being modelled on Tekki Shodan. Thought by some to have originated in China, the horizontal line in which the techniques are performed suggests fighting in a boat, or an alleyway — perhaps even with one's back against the wall. The name Naihanchi was changed by Funakoshi for Tekki and has endured ever since.

The system for explaining the Kata is as follows:

On page 170 you will find a schematic diagram of Tekki Sandan and a picture of the camera used to photograph all the main movements which appear at the top of the following pages. The camera position remains constant and the practitioner begins and ends his Kata facing the camera. If in retreat, when his movements are obscured by his back view, we have photographed him from the side or front and this has been clearly marked.

For many years now, throughout Shotokan Karate, students have been taught to move forward, back, to left or right, or to "45°". This applies to basics, Kata and all six forms of basic Kumite.

In this book, to assist in the explanation of Kata, as far as DIRECTION is concerned, I have likened these moves to the points of the compass.

At the top left hand side of page 170 will be found a photograph of a compass showing the four cardinal points of North, South, East and West, together with the four lesser ones of South East, South West, etc. Eight in all — the same eight that cover almost every Shotokan move taught today.

On the top right hand side of the page is a simplified version showing the eight directions. With the practitioner standing in the centre, facing the camera, forward is "One", back is "Two", his left is "Three", and his right "Four".

Once this simple eight point system has been grasped, the most advanced Kata can be easily understood — directionally speaking.

To summarize then — the photograph at the top of the page is the completed move.

The photographs in the centre of the page show the completed moves, possibly at different angles, to aid understanding, plus the midway points. Finally, the practical application is shown at the bottom of the page and a complete summary of Tekki Sandan appears on page 190.

There is no substitute for a good teacher and this book is merely intended to complement that teaching — not replace it.

The following ten elements of Kata, as taught by Kanazawa Sensei, should be borne in mind at all times. Without them, the Kata will be meaningless.

YOI NO KISIN — the spirit of getting ready. The concentration of will and mind against the opponent as a preliminary to the movements of the Kata.

INYO — the active and passive. Always keeping in mind both attack and defence.

CHIKARA NO KYOJAKU — the manner of using strength. The degree of power used for each movement and position in Kata.

WAZA NO KANKYU — the speed of movement. The speed used for each movement and position in Kata.

TAI NO SHINSHUKU — the degree of expansion or contraction. The degree of expansion or contraction of the body in each movement and position in Kata.

KOKYU — breathing. Breath control related to the posture and movement in Kata*.

TYAKUGAN — the aiming points. In Kata you must keep the purpose of the movement in mind.

KIAI — shouting. Shouting at set points in Kata to demonstrate the martial spirit.

KEITAI NO HOJI — correct positioning. Correct positioning in movement and stance.

ZANSHIN — remaining on guard. Remaining on guard at the completion of the Kata (i.e. back to 'Yoi') until told to relax 'Enoy'.

*N.B. KOKYU — Breathing in Kata plays a very important part towards its correct execution. Inhalation takes place via the nose and exhalation through the mouth. In the following Kata, where a "sequence" of techniques occurs, inhalation is immediately followed by exhalation spread over the number of techniques involved, which often are performed in rapid succession.

鉄騎三段

"MIGI SOETE JŌDAN URA ZUKI"

SCHEMATIC DIAGRAM
OF TEKKI SANDAN
AND DIRECTIONAL ANALYSIS

MOVE	DIRECTION
1	1
2	1
3	1
4	1
5	1
6	1
7	1
8	4
9	4
10	4
11	1
12	1
13	1
14	1
15	1
16	3
17	1
18	1
19	1
20	1
21	1
22	3
23	3
24	3
25	3
26	1
27	1
28	4
29	4
30	4
31	1
32	1
33	1

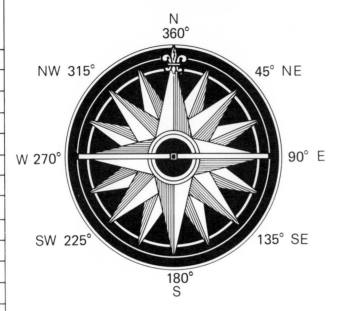

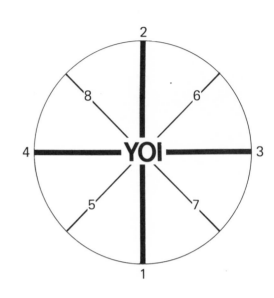

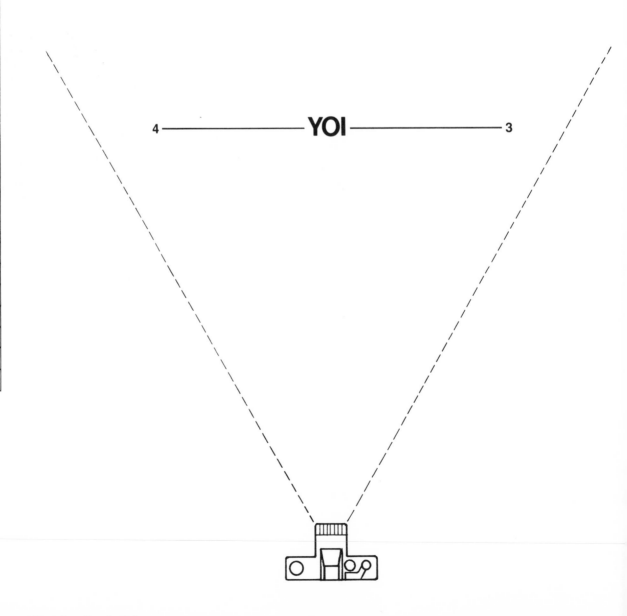

REI

YOI

REI

MIDWAY

YOI

Although Tekki Sandan is an advanced form, the Yoi position is the same as the Heian Katas — that of Shizentai.
After bowing in Heisoku Dachi, move the right leg to the right into Shizentai, breathing in and out in the process.

MOVEMENT 1

HIDARI CHŪDAN UCHI UKE

MOVEMENT 2

KŌSA UKE

YOI

MIDWAY

HIDARI CHŪDAN UCHI UKE

MIDWAY

MOVEMENT 1
Hidari Chūdan Uchi Uke

STANCE: Kiba Dachi.

SHIFT 1: Moving the right leg to the right, bring the left arm under the right and perform a left inside forearm block.

SPEED: Fast with focus.

BREATHING: In through nose — out through mouth.

DIRECTION:

MOVEMENT 2
Kōsa Uke

STANCE: Kiba Dachi.

SHIFT 2: Cross both arms in a semi circular movement, the right one executing an inside forearm block and the left one a downward block (Gedan Barai).

SPEED: Fast with focus.

BREATHING: In through nose — and half out through mouth.

DIRECTION:

YOI

LUNGE PUNCH ATTACK

REVERSE PUNCH ATTACK

YOKO UDE HASAMI

**MIGI JŌDAN NAGASHI UKE
HIDARI MIZUNAGARE NO KAMAE**

KŌSA UKE

MIDWAY

YOKO UDE HASAMI

MIDWAY

MOVEMENT 3
Yoko Ude Hasami

STANCE: Kiba Dachi.

SHIFT 3: Bending the left arm at the elbow, bring it into the horizontal position, at the same time allowing the right forearm to come down on top of it, so catching the punching attack between the arms.

SPEED: Fast with focus.

BREATHING: Half out through mouth.

DIRECTION:

1

MOVEMENT 4
Migi Jōdan Nagashi Uke Hidari Mizunagare No Kamae

STANCE: Kiba Dachi.

SHIFT 4: Without moving the left arm withdrawn the right arm up near to the right ear as illustrated.

SPEED: Fast with focus.

BREATHING: In through nose.

DIRECTION:

1

TRAPPING THE CHUDAN ZUKI BETWEEN THE ARMS

PUNCHING TO THE MID SECTION OR DEFLECTING A REVERSE PUNCH WITH A SWEEPING BLOCK

COUNTER ATTACKING WITH AN UPPER CLOSE PUNCH

MIGI JŌDAN URA ZUKI

RYŪSUI NO KAMAE

MIGI JŌDAN NAGASHI UKE HIDARI MIZUNAGARE NO KAMAE

MIDWAY

MIGI JŌDAN URA ZUKI

MIDWAY

MOVEMENT 5
Migi Jōdan Ura Zuki

STANCE: Kiba Dachi.

SHIFT 5: Thrust the right fist forward in a straight line to attack with an inverted fist punch. Augment the punch by bringing the left back fist to the right elbow.

SPEED: Fast with focus.

BREATHING: Out through mouth.

DIRECTION:

MOVEMENT 6
Ryūsui No Kamae

STANCE: Kiba Dachi.

SHIFT 6: Opening the left hand, palm down, withdraw the right fist to the waist.

SPEED: Fast — no power.

BREATHING: In through nose.

DIRECTION:

ATTACKER STEPS BACK SO AVOIDING A PUNCHING ATTACK . . .

THEN STEPS BACK IN GRASPING THE PUNCHING ARM

SOESHŌ CHŪDAN ZUKI

SOESHŌ KAESHI UDE

RYŪSUI NO KAMAE   MIDWAY

**SOESHŌ
CHŪDAN ZUKI**   MIDWAY

MOVEMENT 7
Soeshō Chūdan Zuki

STANCE: Kiba Dachi.

SHIFT 7: Perform a right middle punch bringing the left hand to the crook of the right arm in an augmenting capacity.

SPEED: Fast with focus.

BREATHING: Half out through mouth.

DIRECTION:

MOVEMENT 8
Soeshō Kaeshi Ude

STANCE: Kiba Dachi.

SHIFT 8: Bend the right arm at the elbow pulling it back to the 45° position. At the same time inverting the fist and sharply turning the head to the right.

SPEED: Fast with focus.

BREATHING: Half out through mouth.

DIRECTION: Body facing 1, head facing 4.

**PULLING THE RIGHT ARM BACK TO THE 45°
POSITION AND BREAKING THE GRIP**

Tekki Sandan   **175**

MIGI SOKUMEN GEDAN UCHI UDE UKE

MIGI SOKUMEN TETTSUI OTOSHI UCHI

SOESHŌ KAESHI UDE

MIDWAY

MIGI SOKUMEN GEDAN UCHI UDE UKE

MIDWAY

MIDWAY

MOVEMENT 9
Migi Sokumen Gedan Uchi Ude Uke

STANCE: Kiba Dachi.

SHIFT 9: Step across to the right with the left leg and then out into straddle stance with the right leg. Swing both arms together to the right and perform an augmented lower forearm block.

SPEED: The first half of the technique is performed fast with half power, the second half fast with focus and full power.

BREATHING: Long inhalation fast exhalation.

DIRECTION: 4

MOVEMENT 10
Migi Sokumen Tettsui Otoshi Uchi

STANCE: Kiba Dachi.

SHIFT 10: Keeping the left hand in position, describe a circle with the right arm, as big as possible, striking with a downward bottom fist strike.

SPEED: Fast with focus.

BREATHING: In through nose, out through mouth.

DIRECTION: 4

BLOCKING A FRONT KICK

USING "KAKE UKE" TO BLOCK A REVERSE PUNCH

CONTINUING THE RIGHT ARM IN A CIRCULAR MOTION . . .

SOESHŌ HIKITE

SOESHŌ MIGI CHŪDAN ZUKI

MIGI SOKUMEN TETTSUI OTOSHI UCHI

MIDWAY

SOESHŌ HIKITE

MIDWAY

MOVEMENT 11
Soeshō Hikite

STANCE: Kiba Dachi.

SHIFT 11: Withdraw the right fist to the waist, simultaneously moving the left hand to the palm down horizontal position as pictured.

SPEED: Half power — fast with focus.

BREATHING: In through nose.

DIRECTION:

MOVEMENT 12
Soeshō Migi Chūdan Zuki

STANCE: Kiba Dachi.

SHIFT 12: Perform a right augmented middle punch.

SPEED: Fast with focus.

BREATHING: Partially out through mouth.

DIRECTION:

AND ATTACKING THE COLLAR BONE WITH AN AUGMENTED DOWNWARD BOTTOM FIST STRIKE

Tekki Sandan   **177**

KŌSA UKE

KŌSA UKE

12

13

SOESHŌ MIGI CHŪDAN ZUKI | MIDWAY | **KŌSA UKE** | MIDWAY

MOVEMENT 13
Kōsa Uke

STANCE: Kiba Dachi.

SHIFT 13: Making a fist with the left hand, bring it to the right ear and then describe a semi circle with both arms culminating with a right inside forearm block and a left downward block (Kōsa Uke).

SPEED: Fast with focus.

BREATHING: Partially out through mouth.

DIRECTION:

1

MOVEMENT 14
Kōsa Uke

STANCE: Kiba Dachi.

SHIFT 14: Swing both forearms in a semi circle performing Kōsa Uke on the opposite side to movement 13.

SPEED: Fast with focus.

BREATHING: Remainder of breath out through mouth.

DIRECTION:

1

1

2

ATTACKER MOVES OUT OF RANGE OF A MIDDLE PUNCH AND . . .

3

THEN DELIVERS A RIGHT PUNCH TO THE STOMACH

HIDARI JŌDAN URA ZUKI

YOKO SASHI ASHI

14

KŌSA UKE

MIDWAY

15

HIDARI JŌDAN URA ZUKI

MIDWAY

MOVEMENT 15
Hidari Jōdan Ura Zuki

STANCE: Kiba Dachi.

SHIFT 15: Thrusting slightly forward with the right arm in a punching action, withdraw the left arm upwards and backwards to the left ear. Now thrust the left fist forward to attack the chin with an augmented close punch.

SPEED: Fast with focus and Kiai.

BREATHING: In on the first half of the technique whilst performing "Nagashi Uke" and "Gedan Zuki" and then out on "Jōdan Ura Zuki".

DIRECTION:

1

MOVEMENT 16
Yoko Sashi Ashi

STANCE: Kōsa Dachi.

SHIFT 16: Look to the left, maintain the arm position and step with the right leg — across the left foot into Kōsa Dachi, but with the side of the right foot touching the floor — not the ball.

SPEED: Slowly — no power.

BREATHING: Long inhalation through nose.

DIRECTION: 3

4

THE FOLLOWS THE STRAIGHT PUNCH WITH A REVERSE PUNCH, WHICH IS BLOCKED ACCORDINGLY . . .

5

AND FOLLOWS IT WITH ANOTHER STRAIGHT PUNCH, THIS TIME AIMED AT THE HEAD

6

HAVING SWEPT THE REVERSE PUNCH ASIDE — DELIVER A LEFT CLOSE PUNCH TO THE CHIN.   179

SOETE URAKEN GAMAE DŌJI FUMIKOMI

YOKO UDE HASAMI

**KŌSA DACHI —
YOKO SASHI ASHI**

MIDWAY

**SOETE URAKEN GAMAE
DŌJI FUMIKOMI**

MIDWAY

MOVEMENT 17
Soete Uraken Gamae Dōji Fumikomi

STANCE: Kiba Dachi.

SHIFT 17: Swing the left leg up and down into Dōji Fumikomi, leaving the arms in prepared position to strike with "backfist".

SPEED: Fast with focus.

BREATHING: Half out through mouth.

DIRECTION:

1

MOVEMENT 18
Yoko Ude Hasami

STANCE: Kiba Dachi.

SHIFT 18: Without moving the right arm, bring the left forearm down horizontally on to it so trapping the attacking punch.

SPEED: Fast with focus.

BREATHING: Remaining half of breath out.

DIRECTION:

1

BLOCKING "UCHI UKE"

STRIKING WITH BACKFIST

TRAPPING THE REVERSE PUNCH

HIDARI JŌDAN URA ZUKI

RYŪSUI NO KAMAE

YOKO UDE HASAMI

MIDWAY

HIDARI JŌDAN URA ZUKI

MIDWAY

MOVEMENT 19
Hidari Jōdan Ura Zuki

STANCE: Kiba Dachi.

SHIFT 19: Only move the left arm, by pulling it back near to the left ear and thrusting it directly forward to administer a left upper close punch. N.B. The action of the left arm pulling back, deflects in a sweeping action, an upper punching attack.

SPEED: Fast with focus.

BREATHING: In through nose, out through mouth.

DIRECTION:

MOVEMENT 20
Ryūsui No Kamae

STANCE: Kiba Dachi.

SHIFT 20: Pulling the left inverted fist to the waist, simultaneously open the right hand.

SPEED: Fast — no power.

BREATHING: In through nose.

DIRECTION:

SWEEPING ASIDE AN UPPER PUNCH . . .

AND STRIKING THE CHIN WITH A CLOSE PUNCH

SOESHŌ HIDARI CHŪDAN ZUKI

SOESHŌ KAESHI UDE

20

RYŪSUI NO KAMAE   MIDWAY

21

SOESHŌ HIDARI
CHŪDAN ZUKI   MIDWAY

MOVEMENT 21
Soeshō Hidari Chudan Zuki

STANCE: Kiba Dachi.

SHIFT 21: Perform a left middle punch bringing the right hand into the crook of the left elbow.

SPEED: Fast with focus.

BREATHING: Half through mouth.

DIRECTION:

1

MOVEMENT 22
Soeshō Kaeshi Ude

STANCE: Kiba Dachi.

SHIFT 22: Bend the left arm at the elbow pulling it back to the 45° position, at the same time inverting the fist and sharply turning the head to the left.

SPEED: Fast with focus.

BREATHING: Remaining half of breath out through mouth.

DIRECTION:

3

1 PUNCHING TO THE MID SECTION

2 ATTACKER GRABS PUNCHING ARM

3 PULLING BACK AND BREAKING THE GRIP

YOKO SASHI ASHI

SOKUMEN HIDARI GEDAN UCHI UDE UKE

SOESHŌ KAESHI UDE

22

MIDWAY

YOKO SASHI ASHI

23

MIDWAY

MOVEMENT 23
Yoko Sashi Ashi

STANCE: Kōsa Dachi — but with the side of the right foot touching the floor.

SHIFT 23: Step to the left with the right foot and just cross over the left one, keeping the arms in the same position as movement 22.

SPEED: Slowly — no power.

BREATHING: Long inhalation through nose.

DIRECTION: 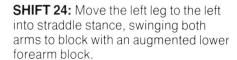 3

MOVEMENT 24
Sokumen Hidari Gedan Uchi Ude Uke

STANCE: Kiba Dachi.

SHIFT 24: Move the left leg to the left into straddle stance, swinging both arms to block with an augmented lower forearm block.

SPEED: Fast with focus.

BREATHING: Out through mouth.

DIRECTION: 3

1

BLOCKING A FRONT KICK ATTACK

2

ATTACKER GRABS THE BLOCKING ARM AT THE WRIST

3

PULLING BACK — BREAKING THE GRIP AND COUNTER ATTACKING WITH A BOTTOM FIST STRIKE TO THE HEAD

HIDARI SOKUMEN TETTSUI OTOSHI UCHI

SOESHŌ HIKITE

SOKUMEN HIDARI GEDAN UCHI UDE UKE

MIDWAY

MIDWAY

HIDARI SOKUMEN TETTSUI OTOSHI UCHI

MIDWAY

MOVEMENT 25
Hidari Sokumen Tettsui Otoshi Uchi

STANCE: Kiba Dachi.

SHIFT 25: Keeping the right arm in position, describe a circle with the left arm, as large as possible, striking with a downward bottom fist strike.

SPEED: Fast with focus.

BREATHING: In through nose, out through mouth.

DIRECTION:

MOVEMENT 26
Soeshō Hikite

STANCE: Kiba Dachi.

SHIFT 26: Withdraw the left fist to the waist, at the same time moving the right hand to the palm down horizontal position as pictured.

SPEED: Fast — no power.

BREATHING: In through nose.

DIRECTION:

SOESHŌ HIDARI CHŪDAN ZUKI

MIGI SOKUMEN TATE SHUTŌ UKE

SOESHŌ HIKITE

MIDWAY

SOESHŌ HIDARI CHŪDAN ZUKI

MIDWAY

MOVEMENT 27
Soeshō Hidari Chūdan Zuki

STANCE: Kiba Dachi.

SHIFT 27: Perform a left augmented middle punch.

SPEED: Fast with focus.

BREATHING: Out through mouth.

DIRECTION:

MOVEMENT 28
Migi Sokumen Tate Shutō Uke

STANCE: Kiba Dachi.

SHIFT 28: Move the right arm in an arc, turning the head to the right in time with the arm and complete a right vertical knife hand block.

SPEED: Slowly no power.

BREATHING: Long inhalation through nose.

Direction:

BLOCKING A LUNGE PUNCH WITH A VERTICAL KNIFE HAND BLOCK

SLIDING IN AND COUNTER ATTACKING WITH A HOOK PUNCH

185

HIDARI KAGE ZUKI

YOKO SASHI ASHI

28

**MIGI SOKUMEN
TATE SHUTŌ UKE**

MIDWAY

29

HIDARI KAGE ZUKI

MIDWAY

**MOVEMENT 29
Hidari Kage Zuki**

STANCE: Kiba Dachi.

SHIFT 29: Make a fist with the right hand pulling it sharply to the waist whilst punching with a roundhouse action with the left arm to execute a hook punch.

SPEED: Fast with focus.

BREATHING: Out through mouth.

DIRECTION:

**MOVEMENT 30
Yoko Sashi Ashi**

STANCE: Kōsa Dachi — but with the side of the left foot touching the floor.

SHIFT 30: Maintain the arm position and step with the left leg across the right foot into Kōsa Dachi.

SPEED: Slowly — no power.

BREATHING: Long inhalation through nose.

DIRECTION:

PREPARING TO ATTACK

HIDARI CHŪDAN UCHI UKE, DŌJI FUMIKOMI

KŌSA UKE

YOKO SASHI ASHI

MIDWAY

HIDARI CHŪDAN UCHI UKE — DŌJI FUMIKOMI

MIDWAY

MOVEMENT 31
Hidari Chūdan Uchi, Uke, Dōji Fumikomi

STANCE: Kiba Dachi.

SHIFT 31: Swing the right leg up in front of the body and down into Dōji Fumikomi. The left fist brushes the right ear as the upper body twists to the right and then blocks with an inside forearm block.

SPEED: Fast with focus.

BREATHING: Partially out through mouth.

DIRECTION:

MOVEMENT 32
Kōsa Uke

STANCE: Kiba Dachi.

SHIFT 32: Move both arms in opposite directions in a semi circle to block "Kōsa Uke" (Uchi Uke — Gedan Barai)

SPEED: Fast with focus.

BREATHING: Partially out through mouth.

DIRECTION:

BLOCKING A LUNGE PUNCH WITH "UCHI UKE"   **BLOCKING A REVERSE PUNCH WITH "KOSA UKE"**

MIGI JŌDAN NAGASHI UKE—HIDARI GEDAN ZUKI

MIGI SOETE JŌDAN URA ZUKI

KŌSA UKE

MIDWAY

MIGI JŌDAN NAGASHI UKE—HIDARI GEDAN ZUKI

MIDWAY

MOVEMENT: 33A
Migi Jōdan Nagashi Uke — Hidari Gedan Zuki

STANCE: Kiba Dachi.

SHIFT 33A: Thrusting slightly forward with the left arm in a punching action, withdraw the right arm up and back to the right ear.

SPEED: Fast with focus.

BREATHING: Partially out through mouth.

DIRECTION:

MOVEMENT 33
Migi Soete Jōdan Ura Zuki

STANCE: Kiba Dachi.

SHIFT 33: Thrust the right fist forward in a straight line to attack with an upper augmented close punch.

SPEED: Fast with focus and Kiai.

BREATHING: Remainder of breath out.

DIRECTION:

BLOCKING A STRAIGHT PUNCH WITH "KOSA UKE"

SWEEPING ASIDE AN UPPER REVERSE PUNCH . . .

AND COUNTER ATTACKING WITH A RIGHT UPPER CLOSE PUNCH

YAME

REI

**MIGI SOETE
JŌDAN URA ZUKI**

MIDWAY

YAME

To complete the Kata, return to the "Yame" position by moving the right leg into "Shizentai" at the same time crossing the arms in front of the body, whilst breathing in and out.

To bow, bring the right leg to the left one into "Helsoku Dachi" and "Rei".

TEKKI SANDAN

REI YOI **1** **2**

7 **8** **9** **10**

15 KIAI

16 **17** **18**

23 **24** **25** **26**

31 **32** **33A** **33** KIAI

YAME

REI

"MIGI SOETE JODAN
URA ZUKI"

*A young boy travelled across Japan to the
school of a great and famous swordsman. When
he arrived at the school he was given an audience
with the founder, who was impressed that this
young boy had made such a long journey.*

"What do you wish from me?" the master asked.

*"I wish to be your student and become the
finest swordsman in the land," the boy replied.*

"How long must I study?"

"Ten years at least," the master answered.

*"Ten years is a long time. What if I studied twice as
hard as all your other students?"*

"Twenty years," replied the master.

*"Twenty years! What if I practise unrelentingly,
day and night with all my effort?"*

"Thirty years," replied the master.

*"How is it that each time I say I will work harder
you tell me that it will take longer?" the
student asked, quite confused by now.*

"The answer is clear," said the master.

*"When there is one eye fixed upon your
destination, there is only one eye left with
which to find the way."*

An old Japanese story.

"YOKO UDE HASAMI"

WANKAN

王
冠

IS COMING . . .